MW00460789

A RHYTHM OF LIFE: THE *Monastic* WAY

Brother Victor-Antoine d'Avila-Latourrette

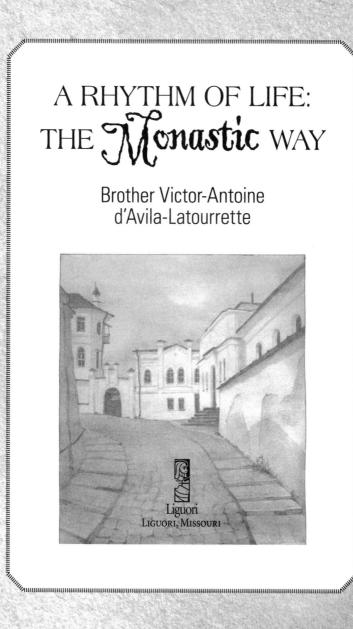

Liguori
LIGUORI, MISSOURI

Imprimi Potest:
Harry Grile, CSsR, Provincial
Denver Province, The Redemptorists

Published by Liguori Publications
Liguori, Missouri 63057

To order, call 800-325-9521, or visit liguori.org

Library of Congress Cataloging-in-Publication Data

D'Avila-Latourrette, Victor-Antoine.
   A rhythm of life : the monastic way / Victor-Antoine d'Avila-Latourrette.
      p. cm.
   Includes bibliographical references.
1. Monastic and religious life. 2. Church year meditations. 3. Devotional calendars—Catholic
Church. I. Title.
   BX2435.D335 2012
   248.8'94—dc23

                                                                          2012028090

p ISBN 978-0-7648-2227-8
e ISBN 978-0-7648-6737-8

The *O Antiphons* section of this book contains text written by Brother Victor-Antoine
d'Avila-Latourrette and published by Liguori Publications in *A Monastery Journey to
Christmas.*

The following sections of this book contain text written by Brother Victor-Antoine d'Avila-
Latourrette and published by Liguori/Triumph in *Blessings of the Daily: Transitus of Saint
Benedict, Solemnity of Saint Benedict,* and *Nativity of the Theotokos.*

Liguori Publications, a nonprofit corporation, is an apostolate of The Redemptorists.
To learn more about The Redemptorists, visit Redemptorists.com.

Printed in the United States of America
16 15 14 13 12 / 5 4 3 2 1
First Edition

CONTENTS

AUTHOR'S NOTE

Throughout my many years in monastic life, I have benefited a great deal from the experience, knowledge, wisdom, and richness of the monastic tradition at large, from that of the East and that of the West. The quotes in this book reflect my particular perspectives and interpretations and are often based on my own direct translations from the French, Spanish, Italian, or Latin versions of texts.

PART 1

THE SOURCES AND

ORIGINS OF

Monastic

LIFE

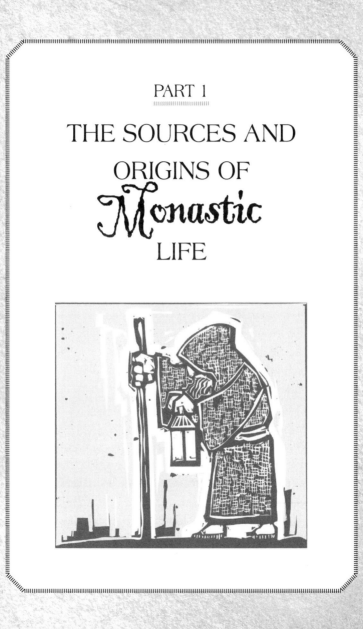

CHAPTER 1
The Origins

The Monk

The monk is one who is separated from all, yet is united to all.
EVAGRIUS PONTICUS, FOURTH-CENTURY MONK, *PRACTIKOS*

I believe that it is the witness of the monk to the eternal, to preach the tenderness of God, and to live it.
MOTHER MARIA, *HER LIFE IN LETTERS*

*M*onk comes from the Greek word *monachos,* meaning "alone." The term applies to one who makes the choice to lead a life that is solitary, unified, integrated, pacified, and undivided in the quest for the absolute. For the sake of God, the monk leaves the world, its allures, pleasures, and all those ties that have been part of his life up until that point. This is painful and hard; after all, monks and nuns have much the same feelings and sensibilities as their fellow human beings. The difference is they have heard a call in their hearts, an inviting call that tells them, "Come. I am the Way, the Truth, and the Life. Follow me." The person who decides to become a monk or nun—to enter the solitude of the desert (a monastery or hermitage)—does it because he or she has heard this call, a call stronger than any other, a call to communion and fullness of life with God, a call that fulfills the deepest desires of the human heart.

He is toil. The monk toils at all he does. That is what a monk is.
ABBA JOHN THE DWARF, *THE SAYINGS OF THE DESERT FATHERS*

Monastic Life: A Mystery

To come face to face with the mystery of a monastic vocation and to grapple with it is a profound experience. To live as a monk is a great gift, not given to many.

JOHN DAIDO LOORI, ROSHI

Monastic life, like any life, remains essentially a mystery. God calls everyone in this world to a particular form of life, and monastic life is precisely a response to a call. The monk's call is to leave everything behind, as Christ invites us to do in the gospel, and to set out to seek God in silence and solitude. Throughout the ages, monastic life has essentially been the experience of the desert. From the early centuries of Christianity, the Holy Spirit has led certain men and women to the wilderness, where they could hear his voice and he could speak to their hearts. In the desert the Lord invites the monk to compunction and true repentance, to continual prayer and adoration, to voluntary silence, to the humble work of conversion of heart, which ultimately leads to the transfiguration of the monk's being by the power of God's love.

Monastic life is often misunderstood by our secular society as well as by many of our fellow Christians. The emphasis on self-denial, seclusion, and an absolute dedication to prayer makes some think that monastic life is a negative form of life. Some people think monks and nuns are odd people who flee from the company of other human beings and from the responsibilities of the world for an unknown reason. The truth, however, is just the opposite. Monks and nuns, and those who, from time to time, have come to share their life in the monastery, know that prayer totally opens their hearts to God and to the needs of their fellow human beings. If they choose to follow the path of self-renunciation, it is simply that they have heard

Christ's invitation to this particular calling. While they retire to the desert of the monastic life to pray continually, monks and nuns also take in their hearts the concerns of all humanity. Prayer vastly expands the dimensions of the human heart, making it capable of containing both God and the entire human family. Monastic prayer, when perfected by grace, leads the monk and the nun to recognize Christ's presence in every human being.

We can expect to spend our whole lives as monks entering deeper and deeper into the mystery of our monastic vocation, which is our life hidden with Christ in God. If we are real monks, we are constantly rediscovering what it means to be a monk, and yet we never exhaust the full meaning of our vocation.

THOMAS MERTON, *THE MONASTIC JOURNEY*

The Desert: The Quest for the Absolute

Christ's three answers to Satan resounded in the silence of the desert; it was therefore here that the monks came in order to hear them again and to receive them as the rule of their monastic life.

PAUL EVDOKIMOV, *THE STRUGGLE WITH GOD*

Christian monastic life had its humble origins in the desert. The first monks went to the desert to seek God and to pursue a life of union with him. The desert was a special place, for it was there, according to biblical accounts, that God revealed himself in all his glory. In the desert at Mount Sinai, God revealed his name to Moses. During the forty years in the desert, the Lord fed his people with manna from above and gave them water from a rock. It was also in the desert that the prophet Elias met God and entered into dialogue with him.

In the New Testament, we see that John the Baptist went to the desert to prepare the way for the Lord. Later, Jesus himself, led by the Holy Spirit, retired to the desert to prepare for the mission for which his Father had sent him. He returned to the desert again and again, to rest and to pray, during the three years of his ministry. And it was in the desert at Mount Tabor, shortly before his passion, that he lifted for a short time the veil of his humanity and revealed to his apostles the splendor of his divinity.

By retiring to the desert, the early monks and nuns were not primarily seeking to renounce all human fellowship. Instead, their aim was to seek God unhindered by the cares of the worldly society of their day. There is no denying that the times of the Desert Fathers were turbulent and confusing (not unlike our own time) and not just in civil society but also in the Church of God. In the midst of all this confusion the clear message of the gospels often became blurred and distorted. The early monks and nuns, following the example of the apostles and martyrs, refused to compromise with the world. They instead sought refuge in the desert, where they could clearly hear the word of God and live by it, with all its consequences. It is in this early desert adventure that the monastic movement originated, and it has ever since been shaped and influenced by it. The call to the solitude of the desert is a constant element in the monastic heart.

However, one thing the Desert Fathers and Mothers (in their deep realism) teach us today is that the desert does not always need to be a geographical place. It can also be found in the solitude and innermost spaces of our hearts. Prayer was the central activity of the desert life, but we can pray anywhere by heeding the gospel's words: "When you pray, go to your inner room, close the door, and pray to your Father in secret" (Matthew 6:6). Continual, unceasing prayer coupled with the daily practice of Christian virtues: charity, humility, obedience, asceticism—these were the ideals for which the desert monks strove in their desert solitude, and which remain valid for monks and Christians of all persuasions today. Ultimately, it means taking both the gospel and our Christian life seriously.

Faithful to this early monastic desert experience, many monasteries are established in isolated places. Today monks often retire for periods of time to a hermitage or take a once-a-week "desert day" in complete solitude, where we are given the opportunity to confront the absolute of God and the crude reality of our own bareness. It is an immense help in the spiritual life. This experience of the desert is so vital to all Christian life that monks and nuns hospitably allow their fellow Christians, and often non-Christians, to partake in the prayer, silence, and solitude of our monasteries.

The desert is fundamentally a state of insecurity. When lost in the desert, this place offers man one objective situation, only one solution: to look to God who redeems us and to wait with complete trust upon him, to abide by an absolute and radical confidence in God alone.

FATHER EDWARD SCHILLEBEECKX, OP

Monasticism: A Gift From the East

Thus, there were in the desert monasteries, which were so many temples filled with heavenly choirs of men who spent their lives singing the psalms, reading the sacred Scriptures, fasting, praying, seeking their consolation in the hope of joys to come, working with their hands in order to give alms, living all together in a perfect charity and a union worthy of admiration. Thus, one could see in these places as it were an altogether different country, cut off from the rest of the world, and the fortunate inhabitants of that country had no other thought than to live in love and justice.

SAINT ATHANASIUS, *LIFE OF SAINT ANTONY*

aint Athanasius describes the life led by the early monks in the Egyptian deserts, but the real origins of the monastic life are in the gospels, in the teachings and example of Jesus himself, and in the prophetic figure of John the Baptist, whose voice cried out in the desert, "Prepare the way of the Lord!" The monastic ideal took root in the early years of Christianity, and it has always remained an integral part of the life of the Church. From the very beginning, there were Christians who took to heart Christ's invitation to leave all they possessed in order to follow him. Obviously, times have changed since Christ first uttered his invitation, but there has never been any lack of those who hear the call, recognize his voice in the depths of their hearts, and feel irresistibly compelled to leave everything behind to follow him.

Since the time of Saint Antony, many have felt the call to that mysterious place called the desert, the "wasteland," always the symbol and reality of total renunciation, where one went to do battle with the forces of evil and to seek God alone with purity of heart. For all monks, those following either the cenobitic or the eremitical life (in a monastic community or as a recluse, respectively), the desert remains the ideal prototype of what monastic life is meant to be: a generous renunciation of evil and not God; a dying to selfishness, so that the true self may emerge; a burning desire and a living thirst for God; and a total fidelity to the smallest commandments of the gospel, so that their lives may be transformed by the power of God's love and transfigured into his likeness.

As the Church was, Christian monasticism was born in the East. This is an important fact to keep in mind as we try to understand monastic life and see its continuity into our time. From the very early days of the Christian Church, there were ascetics and virgins who, while living at home, dedicated themselves to a more rigorous form of Christianity by spending long hours in prayer, practicing fasting, and caring for the poor, the sick, orphans, and widows. In the third century, the first forms of organized monastic life began to appear in Egypt. Attracted by the example of Antony, who had become by then their spiritual father, other Christians began to settle in the desert, eager to be instructed by him. By the time of Antony's death, there were colonies of monks and nuns both in the desert land and also all along the Nile River, seeking God in the footsteps of the humble Father of Monks.

As the number of monks and nuns increased in the desert, the need for a more organized form of monastic life became apparent. At times some of the desert ascetics went to extremes, becoming known for their excesses in penance and other forms of asceticism. As a consequence, they sometimes tended to lose control over the real purpose of their monastic lives.

Just when they were in need of restoring equilibrium, the Lord sent a humble soldier to Tabennisi, a desert village along the east bank of the Nile, with the purpose of reorganizing monastic life in the desert. His conception was a communal form of eremitical life where the brethren could lead lives free from the anxieties and dangers found in the wilderness. The soldier, Pachomius, created the first desert monastery by building a wall around the cells or huts of the monks, protecting them from the world and also joining them to one another. An abbot presided over the community as its head and spiritual mentor, and the monks gathered together weekly for his instruction and for their Sunday worship. The disciples of Pachomius followed a common Rule, wore the same habit, attended the same Offices, and partook of the same work and meals. The discipline and order established by Pachomius in his monasteries enabled the monks to follow a monastic rhythm of life free from the concerns of self and more attuned to the work of God in their souls.

At the same time that Pachomius was establishing monasteries, his sister, Mary, was organizing a community of nuns that could live together in a monastery not far from that of the monks. From the earliest appearance of monastic life in the desert, the presence of women has been felt in its midst. These courageous women's ascetics emulated the monks in their fierce determination to follow Christ, and they often surpassed their brothers in their fidelity and fervor.

The austere monastic life of the monks and nuns in the Egyptian desert became so admired by their fellow Christians that by the late fourth and fifth centuries, it had spread to Palestine, Syria, Armenia, Persia, Cappadocia, Gaul, Spain, and Italy. Late in the fourth century, another prominent monastic figure appeared on the Christian horizon: Basil the Great, a Greek, who was highly educated and was held in high esteem by the emperors, the bishops, and the learned laity. His great contribution to the early monastic movement was to enrich the communal form of monastic life with a solid theological grounding. Saint Basil provided his monastery with a form of legislation called the Longer and the Shorter Rules, which tempered some of the Egyptian monastic practices and thus invited moderately motivated Christians to embrace the monastic state. Basil saw the monastic community, patterned after the example of the early Christians (such as described in Acts 4:32), as the only place in which true Christian ideals could be realized. For Saint Basil, the communal life provided the monks with the opportunity to practice fraternal charity, fulfilling the Lord's commandment to love one another. Saint Basil's Rule was seen as a synthesis of all that was best in the monastic tradition, and it had a great influence both in the East and in the West. A Latin translation of Saint Basil's

Rule, brought to the West early on, served as the guide for many monasteries. The monastic ideal also came to the West via three very important figures: Saint Martin of Tours, Saint John Cassian, and Saint Augustine. They established monastic centers in the West, which fostered both the communal life and the strife for perfection of the individual monk.

These three and Saint Basil were the worthy predecessors of Saint Benedict, the inheritor of the monastic tradition of both the East and the West. Greatly influenced by Saint Basil's Rule, Saint Benedict—founding his monastery at Monte Cassino, seventy-five miles southeast of Rome, in 529—would create in his own Rule the most effective monastic synthesis of Eastern and Western traditions, a synthesis that has been faithfully transmitted for fifteen centuries, to our own days.

Saint Benedict conceived the communal monastic life as "a school in the Lord's service" where monks could work together to attain their salvation and sanctification. For Saint Benedict, the monk enters a monastery solely "to seek God," and in the pursuit of this ideal, he is encouraged by the mutual support and example of the brethren who are there for the same purpose. Saint Benedict showed a great deal of wisdom and common sense in his Rule, pragmatically adapting the Eastern monastic pattern to the needs, customs, and culture of the West. By doing so, he was able to strengthen the community of his monks and make of it a living icon of what the Church of Christ ought to be like. This model of a perfect Christian community was, for Saint Benedict, a reality that had eternal implications.

The resilience and adaptability of the desert ideal to the different circumstances and different ways of life was in fact one of its chief virtues.

Douglas Burton-Christie, *The Word in the Desert*

CHAPTER 2
The Foundations of Monastic Life

The Gospel

See, in His loving kindness, the Lord showeth us the way of life. Therefore, having our loins girt with faith and the performance of good works, let us walk His ways under the guidance of the Gospel, that we may be found worthy of seeing Him who hath called us to His kingdom.

RULE OF SAINT BENEDICT, PROLOGUE

Since the life of the monk consists primarily of the imitation of Christ, the serious reading of, listening to, and study of the gospel becomes the most vital element of his monastic day. He seeks to shape his life by the teachings of Jesus, by trying to follow with integrity and great fidelity even the smallest precepts of the gospel, which leads him to the full knowledge of the revelation of God in Jesus Christ. It allows the monk to grow deeper and deeper into the "living experience" of him who reveals himself to the humble, the poor, the lowly, to the little ones.

Saint Benedict encourages the monk to walk in the steps of the gospel—for him, the monastery is "a school in the Lord's service," where the monk or nun comes to learn to live according to the teachings of the gospel. There is nothing more important to the monk, in the mind of Saint Benedict, than learning to know Christ through his word and then completely identifying with him. According to

Saint Benedict, the monk or nun must assiduously spend several hours a day in *lectio divina*; that is, in reading and meditating on the sacred Scriptures, in particular, the gospels. By fidelity to this practice, the monk brings his whole being, with all its powers and faculties, into a life-giving encounter with the revealed word of God. There illumined by the Holy Spirit, he is nourished in the knowledge of God.

The reading, study, and prayerful pondering of the word of God is a joint action undertaken at the same time by both God and the monk: God speaks and the monk listens. And this interaction between the two is the work of the Holy Spirit.

Practice fasting; then meditate on the Gospel and the other Scriptures, and if an alien thought arises within you, never look at it but always look upwards, and the Lord will come at once to your help.

Macarius the Great, a Desert Father

Following Christ

Jesus said, "If you wish to be perfect, go, sell your possessions, and give the money to the poor, and you will have treasure in heaven; then come, follow me."

Matthew 19:21 (New Revised Standard Version)

These words from the gospel seized the heart of Saint Antony, the first monk, and transformed his life forever. Likewise, Jesus invites us today to follow him into the desert of the monastic life. The monk, touched by grace and seized by the love of Christ, slowly turns away from the ways of the world and wholeheartedly gives himself to following the Lord.

The monastic life, consecrated exclusively to following Christ, is lived in a spirit of great simplicity, humility, and poverty, according to the gospel. The monk wishes to follow the poor Christ and live in solidarity with those who still reveal him to us: the poor, such as the oppressed, the rejected, and the underprivileged people of the world. In his daily life, the monk has concrete ways of living out this identification with the poor, as through his humble manual work. His diet, which includes fasting and abstinence from meat, he joyfully accepts for Christ's sake, mindful that a great many people of the world are starving and are often exploited because of the affluence and waste embraced by society. When he can, he gives individual

assistance to those in need. The spirit of the Beatitudes remains always the ideal for all monks.

For Saint Benedict, obedience is one of the most important ways by which the monk imitates and follows Christ. In Hebrews 5:8–9 we learn that Jesus, "Son though he was, he learned obedience from what he suffered; and when he was made perfect, he became the source of eternal salvation for all who obey him." For the love of Christ, the monk willingly accepts submission to the will of another human being—the abbot, according to *The Rule of Saint Benedict*—sacrificing his own will and desires in order to imitate more completely the example of his master and Savior. It is not the abbot alone, however, that the monk is encouraged to obey. Saint Benedict goes a bit further, inviting the monks to obey one another, thus walking in the steps of Christ: "The brethren must render the service of obedience not only to the Abbot, but they must thus also obey one another, knowing that they shall go to God by this path of obedience" (*The Rule of Saint Benedict*, chapter 71).

The monk hears the Lord's exhortation to lose his own life in order to gain it, and it is in the experience of this paradox that the monk mysteriously finds his ultimate fulfillment.

The great ends of the monastic life can only be seen in the light of the mystery of Christ. Christ is the center of monastic living. He is the source and its end. He is the way of the monk as well as his goal.

THOMAS MERTON, *THE MONASTIC JOURNEY*

The Monastic Tradition

Tradition is the instrument of a perfect koinonia, *communion, both in forms and in spirit, throughout the centuries and across frontiers.*

BISHOP ANTONIE PLOIESTENUL,
LIBERTY AND TRADITION IN ORTHODOX MONASTICISM

The living monastic tradition is such that rich and common inheritance, which monks and nuns have received from the past, continue to live in the present and pass on to future generations. Tradition is the sap of monastic life. Without it, it is impossible to begin to understand this life's mystery.

The monastic tradition is an objective reality and hence authenticates all monastic living. The reason we monks speak of and show such reverence for tradition is that our life is incarnated, so to speak, in a living tradition and cannot be separated from it. This living tradition is the flow of life that has been handed over to us from the sacred Scriptures, particularly the gospels, the teachings of the apostles, the example of the early monks and nuns of the desert, and the continual monastic living throughout the centuries, with its ups and downs. Tradition is both continuity and a direct link to our roots. Tradition is the Holy Spirit's inner dynamic that keeps the monastic life, like the Church, ever ancient yet ever new.

However, as renowned monastic scholar Dom Jean Leclercq often used to remind us, there is Tradition and there are traditions. There is a great deal of misunderstanding in our time about these, and it is vitally important not to confuse them. The monastic tradition that we value is rooted in the word of God, in the example of Jesus, and is what the early monks and nuns inherited from the apostles and the first Christians. Tradition in this sense, conveying perennial gospel values, remains of timeless value to us. Some of these values—like faith, prayer, conversion, humility, charity, simplicity, good works, obedience, and hospitality—are always valid no matter how they are expressed throughout different cultures and times. Traditions, however, are another thing. Mere traditions are, more or less, culturally conditioned customs that originated at certain times and places. They are not essential to the monastic life, as are the values that spring from the gospel. Traditions in and of themselves are not necessarily bad, but it is important to see them in their historical contexts; otherwise, we may fall into danger of canonizing them. This distinction is particularly important for our time, with many people's great tendency toward fundamentalism.

To give one example of the difference between Tradition and traditions, let me speak of something greatly treasured in the life of a monastery, namely the Divine Offices. Up until the time of the last ecumenical council, in Western monasteries the Offices were always celebrated in Latin and sung in the Gregorian chant. However, since the council introduced the use of our vernacular languages into the liturgy, many monasteries have opted likewise, finding that their mother tongue facilitates and strengthens their liturgical prayer.

This option, in the light of Tradition, is completely valid, for those things which are important—prayer and the celebration of God's praises—are retained and hopefully enhanced.

Thus, we see in this case that *Tradition* is upheld, while the *traditions* (Latin and the Gregorian chant) are replaced by other forms. Changes in traditions do not affect the nature of monastic life. It would be something altogether different, however, if the monasteries were to try to substitute prayer and the Offices themselves, which are intrinsic values in the monastic life. That would really be tampering with Tradition. (I do not wish to disparage Latin or the Gregorian chant, which are so dear to many monasteries and are, to some extent, used and retained here in our monastery. However, it is important to point out—even to those of us who retain such values—that these are part of traditions and not of Tradition.) After all, the early monks in the desert, like Antony and Pachomius, did not know Latin, yet they were quite happy praising God in their own tongue.

Saint Antony, the father of monks, was called a true inheritor of the fire of the Pentecost, for he was a man filled with the Holy Spirit. What we monks and nuns call the living monastic tradition is the precious pearl of the gospel, an inheritance we have received from our ancient fathers and mothers, an inheritance which contains within itself life in the Holy Spirit, a life filled with fire and love, capable of being transmitted again and again to every generation.

If we want to live as monks, we must try to understand what the monastic life really is. We must try to reach the springs from which that life flows. We must have some notions of our spiritual roots, that we may be better able to sink them deep into the soil.

Thomas Merton, *The Monastic Journey*

The Rule of Saint Benedict

The Rule is always more than a code of life or a manual of doctrine, although it is both of these. It is above all a résumé of a spiritual experience that lies at the heart of the monastic life. The principles of doctrines it evokes, or the details of obedience which are recommended or even imposed by it, have an inner power. This power is an experience of the very life of God in Christ Jesus and his Holy Spirit.

The letter of the Rule contains life within itself, and this life can be awakened in the heart of the disciple. Hence the importance of the very opening words of the Rule: "Listen, O my son."

Dom Andre Louf, *The Cistercian Way*

Saint Benedict tells us in chapter 73, the last chapter of the Rule, that he wrote the Rule for beginners. Since the sixth century, innumerable monks and nuns have lived by it, still doing so in diverse cultural settings and across all continents. The Rule has survived the passing of time and has inspired monks and nuns throughout the ages—proof of its universal appeal, wisdom, and certainly its timeless validity. Thousands of books and articles have been written about the Rule, by both monks and scholars who have studied the Rule from every possible angle. Indeed, the great number of new books and commentaries on the subject that appear every year never ceases to amaze me.

Many young students come to our monastery showing interest in monasticism. Some ask me why the Rule appeals to people in this technological twenty-first century. What does a sixth-century document have to say to people so removed in culture and time from Saint Benedict?

The Rule can be appreciated for various reasons, but one that particularly appeals to me is its wise latitude in the way it encourages us monks to walk in the footsteps of the gospel. The Rule tacitly acknowledges a certain pluralism, making general points instead of specific ones about many observances, allowing for creativity and improvement, where this is possible. The Rule is not limited to its original place and time; like the gospels, from which it draws its inspiration, it has wisdom as alive and full of meaningful implications today as it was at the time the Rule was composed.

A second reason for the Rule's continuing appeal is its deep connection to individual persons. From the first words of the prologue, "Listen, O my son," Saint Benedict's great love for the reader is evident. It is to him that Saint Benedict addresses the words of life of the Rule, thus passing on the grace, the wisdom, and the richness of his own experience. It is then up to the individual monk to embrace the Rule as a way of life, distilling wisdom day by day from it.

A third element in the Rule that retains a timeless appeal to monks is the perfect pattern it creates for the monastic day. The Rule prescribes an equal distribution of time among prayer, sacred reading, intellectual work, manual work, and rest, thus bringing into balance all the activities of the monastic day. Saint Benedict was a genius in establishing through the Rule a way of life where the seasons of the earth, with their sequences of darkness and light, and the seasons of the Christian liturgy come into harmonious consonance, thus giving a dynamic balance and a healing rhythm to the monk's daily life.

The Rule, a perfect synthesis of what is best in the traditions of the East and the West, remains a living guide to the monastic journey. Every day we read a portion of the Rule in the monastery, and we find its teachings alive with meaning and purpose. When the postulant enters the novitiate, the monk in charge of training him daily opens the novice's eyes and heart to the truth and treasures contained in the Rule. Slowly, the novice learns to walk the path traced by the Rule, and he eventually finds there a quiet, hidden source of strength, sustaining and encouraging him throughout his inner journey. Through the reading and daily living out of the Rule, the presence and example of Saint Benedict remains alive in the monastery and in the heart of the monk. The Rule is life-giving and consequently has the power to transmit this life from one generation of monks to another.

In his Rule, Saint Benedict did not seek to present a theory of the spiritual life, but simply to offer a practical program for persons wanting to live the Christian life fully. Nevertheless, all his specific directives are backed by clear insight into the essence and the mysteries of the spiritual life. This insight was deepened by years of intensive study of Holy Scripture, ecclesiastical writers, and monastic pioneers. It was confirmed and crowned by the experience of coming to know all the stages of the way to God in his own search and struggle.

DOM EMMANUEL HEUFELDER, *THE WAY TO GOD*

To Seek God Above All

Imagine that there is nothing else in front of your eyes—as though you were not among mankind—because you are seeing nothing else but God, for God is the entire reason for your way of life.

JOHN THE SOLITARY, *THE SYRIAC FATHERS*

$\mathcal{S}$aint Benedict structured his Rule in such a way as to indicate that the sole purpose for the monastic vocation is to seek God above all. In the monastery or hermitage, the monk must not waste time or energy seeking human approval. Only God's approval matters. Saint Benedict measures the advances a monk makes in his spiritual quest by the level of detachment from earthly approvals, popularity, contests, and especially by the degree of the monk's self-surrender into the Father's loving hands. For Saint Benedict, to seek God alone means to abandon one's former life completely, as Jesus did, and to entrust oneself to the Father's will. While Jesus was making his entrance into our world, he uttered: "Behold, I come to do thy will." During his earthly days he prayed daily, humbly: "Thy will be done on earth as it is in heaven."

There is definitely a certain pedagogy in the Rule. Saint Benedict wishes to show the monk that, just as Jesus lived for God alone

and sought him above all, the monk must act likewise in his daily monastic search. After all, the disciple is no greater than the master. This implies that the example of the master defines the path the disciple must follow. All authentic monastic life is thoroughly theocentric. Just as Jesus committed his life radically to God alone, even to the point of death on the cross, so must the monk commit himself to a life of full communion with God in all times and in all places. Prayer is the monk's daily tool in his search for fullness of life with God. The Holy Spirit, through continual prayer, guides the heart of the monk toward the living waters of God's love. Only when we begin to love God as he really is, above all things, do we discover the true joy that can replenish all the desires of the human heart. No other but God can fully satisfy the human heart. In the words of Saint Augustine: "Our hearts are restless, Lord, and they cannot find rest until they rest in You."

CHAPTER 3
Aspects of Monastic Life

The Monastery

The paths leading to the monastery are diverse. But one day they will converge and form a single way, meeting in him who said, "I am the Way," and, "No one can come to the Father except through me." The Christian who becomes a monk is seeking no other way than this. What he makes his own is what he has seen and heard in the words and deeds of Jesus. As Saint Benedict said in the Prologue to his Rule for monasteries, "Let us set out on this way with the Gospel for our guide...." In saying this, Saint Benedict is saying no more than Saint John, who said, "We must live the same kind of life that Christ lived."

Dom André Louf, *The Cistercian Way*

aint Benedict conceived the purpose of a monastery to be "a school in the Lord's service"; that is to say, a school of life where the monk is taught to live by the teachings of the gospel and is shown the path to salvation. The monastery is the training ground where the monk learns to orient his whole life toward rendering fitting service to the Lord. A monastery, as all schools are, is located in a definite place and comprises a church and buildings like a dormitory or cells, cloister, refectory, library, scriptorium, chapter room, parlors, and workrooms. There are usually also gardens, orchards, and farm buildings within the monastic enclosure. The monastery is a home to the monk, and by his vow of stability, he becomes permanently attached to this home, to his monastic community, and to the physical locality, where he will spend the rest of his days in God's service.

A monastery is a school where the monk is taught different subjects:

School of Prayer: A monastery is a place where the monk learns to seek the living God. Prayer is the natural expression of this seeking, so the monk cultivates the art of prayer as his life's sole purpose. Several times during the day, the monk is summoned by bells to the Oratory to sing the *Opus Dei*, the praises of God. Prolonged periods are given to private, solitary prayer. Continual prayer is sought by frequent recourse to prayer in the name of Jesus.

School of Silence: The deep monastic silence is the ordinary ambiance where the monk reads, studies, and is nourished by the word of God. The silence of a monastery helps to create a unique quality of life, a creative stillness in which the monk and those who share his life are able to experience God and to begin to grasp the mystery of their existence.

School of Work: Imitating the life of Christ, the monk leads a simple, poor, and laborious life. The monk lives by the work of his hands, which allows him to live in solidarity with his fellow human beings, especially the poor and the oppressed. The monk's work is connected with the flow of the seasons and the rhythm of creation. Special reverence is given to the cultivation of the land and to animal farming. Conservation, recycling, frugality, and austerity are aspects of the monastic lesson of cooperation with utmost respect for the mystery of God's creation.

School of Fraternal Life: Guided by the Rule, the monastic community is a stable family unit centered on the abbot, who "is believed to be the representative of Christ in the monastery." As the early

Christians were, the monastic community strives to be "of one heart and mind" (Acts 4:32).

School of Conversion to Christ: Moved by the Holy Spirit and the desire to live in closer communion with Christ, the monk vows obedience, conversion, and stability to a particular monastery. There he seeks to imitate the hidden life of Christ through obedience, humility, prayer, work, fasting, and keeping vigils. The monk denies himself daily in order to follow Christ (Rule, chapter 4).

School of the Heart: Saint Benedict, taking after Saint John Cassian and the early monastic tradition, envisions the monastic ideal as "seeking God with purity of heart." Jesus makes purity of heart one of the Beatitudes: "Blessed are the pure in heart, for they will see God" (Matthew 5:8, *NRSV*). The monk begins here and now to behold the face of God, which he will see for all eternity. Purity of heart is a necessary condition for union with God and, consequently, for progress in the life of prayer. Purity of heart allows the monk to be docile and receptive to the inspirations of the Holy Spirit and his gift of wisdom, and it gives the monk intuition and a foretaste of divine things.

School of Peace: "*Pax*" is the motto of every Benedictine monastery. It expresses perfectly the ideal of monastic life according to Saint Benedict, for whom the monastery is an abode of peace, for there dwell those who seek the God of peace. The monk strives daily for the harmony and the organic unity that existed at the beginning of creation.

School of Learning, Culture, and the Arts: The tradition of scholarship and culture among the Benedictines is well known, and its decisive influence in the shaping of civilization in Europe has been established. Faithfully guarding the patrimony of this tradition, the monastery zealously encourages the monk toward a "love of learning" and the appreciation and development of culture. Not only is the monk encouraged to study, to work, and to do research, he is also encouraged to enter into dialogue with the many scholars, scientists, artists, craftsmen, writers, and workers who come to the monastery attracted by the values, wisdom, and unity of the monastic life. The cultivation of beauty and the arts, especially in their relation to the worship of God, takes a preeminent place in a monastery. Among the art forms, music has particular importance, for it is integrated in daily prayers.

School of Service: Through the ancient practice of monastic hospitality, the monk shares his life with his fellow men. According to the monastic tradition, the doors of a monastery are to be open to all who seek the peace of God. Amidst the agitation, the noise, and the fast pace of daily living, monasteries offer "spaces of silence" and also the "experience of the desert" so vital for all those wishing to enter into living contact with Christ and renew their friendship with him.

Saint Benedict says that it must be ascertained of a novice whether he is truly seeking God, and he describes the monastery as a school in the Lord's service. And indeed, the monk may well be likened to a student engaged in the most thrilling piece of research work which could be imagined. He cannot tell where it will lead him. Sometimes it is as if he is out on a wide uncharted sea, knowing that though he sees no shore in sight, yet his course is straight and clear before him, because God is the sovereign owner of ship and shore and sea.

Sister Katherine, *A Threefold Cord*

The Abbot: Father of the Community

The Abbot who is worthy to be over a monastery, ought always to be mindful of what he is called, and make his works square with his name of Superior. For he is believed to hold the place of Christ in the monastery, when he is called by his name, according to the saying of the Apostle: "You have received the spirit of adoption of sons, whereby we cry Abba (Father)" (Romans 8:15). Therefore, the Abbot should never teach, prescribe, or command (which God forbid) anything contrary to the laws of the Lord; but his commands and teaching should be instilled like a leaven of divine justice into the minds of his disciples.

RULE OF SAINT BENEDICT, CHAPTER 2

Saint Benedict sees the monastery as "a school in the Lord's service" where the monk comes to be formed with the monastic community as a real, stable family centered on the abbot, the father of the community. He envisions in the community the harmony of an ideal family, where the brethren mutually support each other and where the father leads them wisely and prudently in their quest for God.

In the monastic tradition, the role of the abbot is much more than just the juridical figure the superior is in other religious communities. In fact, there is no parallel there. For Saint Benedict, the abbot "takes the place of Christ" in the community, and it is around him that the stable fraternal relationships of the monastic family are built. With his example and teaching, the abbot encourages the monks to love one another as brothers, practicing charity in forbearance, patience, and mutual respect. Everything done in the monastery is under his direction and with his consent.

Saint Benedict's conception of the monastic community as a family helps us understand the Benedictine vow of stability. Because the monk is part of a permanent, concrete family, he vows stability to the particular monastery of his profession until death. This helps the monk to surrender "mobility"—one of the physical expressions of pride, independence, and self-will—to the healing yoke of obedi-

ence. Stability to a particular monastic family brings to the monk's heart the gifts of security, inner peace, and joy in the Holy Spirit.

Saint Benedict, being both a very spiritual and a practical man, counsels the abbot to form and instruct the monastic community not only with words but also by his good behavior. In the Rule he prescribes, "When, therefore, anyone taketh the name of Abbot he should govern his disciples by a twofold teaching; namely, he should show them all that is good and holy by his deeds more than by his words; explain the commandments of God to intelligent disciples by words, but show the divine precepts to the dull and simple by his works" (chapter 2). Saint Benedict makes it abundantly clear that the abbot must be to his disciples a living example of holiness, and he assures the abbot that his example of holiness and fidelity to Christ at the end would do more for the spiritual welfare of the brethren than all the sermons preached with the most gifted eloquence.

Saint Benedict laid the obligation on all, brothers and abbot, to follow the Rule. At all times and especially in periods of universal decline, the community and the abbot have no better safeguard than a religious respect for an untouchable Rule. An abbot is nothing without a Rule.

Dom Adalbert de Vogüe, *The Rule of Saint Benedict*

The Monastic Habit

Let the habit of the monk be such as may cover the body and protect the monk from the cold... and not such as may foster the seeds of vanity or please the fancy. The habit should be so plain and ordinary, so that it may not be thought remarkable for novelty of color or fashion among other men of the same profession.

SAINT JOHN CASSIAN, *CENOBITIC INSTITUTIONS*

The way the monk dresses signifies, therefore, what he is. Much more, it partially constitutes his very monastic being. From this fact springs the moderate but serious attention which ancient monks constantly gave to their dress.

DOM ADALBERT DE VOGUE, *THE RULE OF SAINT BENEDICT*

The monastic habit is the monk's sign of consecration to God and a reminder to himself of having accepted a life of self-renunciation. To embrace the monastic life, according to Saint Benedict, is to embrace a continual state of repentance and conversion. To the monk, the monastic habit is the quiet symbol of his continual desire for conversion.

Saint Benedict, having received the monastic tradition from the East, attaches the same importance to the monastic habit as the early Desert Fathers did, but he is full of common sense about it: "Let clothing be given to the brethren according to the circumstances of the place and the nature of the climate in which they live, because in cold regions more is needed, while in warm regions less....We believe that for a temperate climate a cowl and a tunic for each monk are sufficient—a woolen cowl for winter and a thin or worn one for summer, and a scapular for work, and stockings and shoes as covering for the feet." Not only is Saint Benedict practical about the habit, he is also full of gospel frugality about the way to go about obtaining the material for it. "Let the monks not worry about the color or the texture of all these things, but let them be such as can be bought more cheaply" (*Rule*, chapter 55). The monk must apply the same standards of simplicity to the habit and his personal dress code as he does to other aspects of his monastic life.

In recent times there has been a tendency in some religious circles to abandon the religious habit and adopt a more secular way of dressing. After all, "the habit does not make the monk," say some of the people who promote this view. While this may be partly true, the opposite is also true, that the wearing of the habit helps make the monk. I think it is important not to confuse the adaptation made by members of active congregations to secular standards, perhaps needed because of the nature of their apostolic work, and then apply the same principles to monastic life. Religious life, as it has evolved in the Western church, and monastic life, as it has always been in both the Eastern and the Western churches, are two different entities, with very different lifestyles and distinct goals. What is of value to one is not necessarily to the other. Thus, the inner renewal demanded of each of them must proceed differently. It does a great injustice to both to try to apply exactly the same standards of renewal to both groups, when the vocations and purposes of the groups are different. Active religious orders like the Franciscans and Jesuits may find it more suited to their traditions to dress like their contemporaries (Saint Francis probably would have been perfectly at home wearing a poor worker's blue jeans today). The monk, however, cannot renounce the monastic habit without sacrificing something very intrinsic to the monastic tradition. Monastic life is an organic whole; monks don't randomly pick and choose what elements in their life they should change according to the fashion of the world. The question of adapting secular standards in order to be relevant to the world is irrelevant to the monk, for his life is meant to be a poor and humble one hidden with Christ in God, not a success story in the eyes of the world. Perhaps paradoxically, in doing this the monk can make his only claim to relevance.

The religious garment in the active orders was not necessarily a habit but a uniform; and until recently, its meaning was that those wearing it belonged to a particular order or institute. Not so with the monastic habit. Saint Benedict, basing his writing on the subject on the teachings of Saint Basil, gives personal nuance to the value of the habit. The monk, being a weak man, needs a constant reminder of his conversion and resolution to lead a perfect life. The habit therefore is not a sign to help others distinguish the wearer. The value of the monastic habit is personal, it is for the monk himself; in fact, it symbolizes the soul of the monk. The monastic habit creates the visible separation between the world the monk renounces and the new life of asceticism he embraces. Moreover, the monastic habit not only reminds the monk of the life of conversion and repentance that he embraces daily; it is also a sign of his belonging to God alone. The monastic habit, in a sense, is a symbol of the wedding garment of the gospel, which tells the monk that he must be prepared at all times for the wedding feast, for the Bridegroom "comes as a thief in the night," and we know neither the day nor the hour. All we know is that we must wear the proper attire to be able to enter the wedding feast.

It was understood in early monasticism that the gesture by which the elder clothed the new monk with the monastic habit on the day of his profession was the sign of the transmission of a spiritual grace inherited from all the monks that preceeded him.

Pere Placide Deseille, *L'echelle de Jacop et la Vision de Dieu*

The monastic habit has the twofold purpose of warning people in the world what to expect of the man who is wearing it, and of warning the man who is wearing it that he must behave in a particular way.

DOM HUBERT VAN ZELLER, *THE HOLY RULE*

Stability

A brother came to the desert of Scetis to visit Abba Moses and asked him for a word. The old man said to him, "Go, sit in your cell, and your cell will teach you everything."

ABBA MOSES, APOTHEGM 6

How difficult it is for us, and for our contemporaries in the twenty-first century, to conceive the idea of staying put in one place for a definite period of time. For most people this would be totally unacceptable. How could we ever relinquish our freedom or mobility? How could we forfeit our desire to see new things and explore new places?

Yet, Abba Moses—with the rest of the Desert Fathers and mothers—tells us precisely to stay within the boundaries of one place. They know that in order to truly explore the territories of the inner journey, the discipline of stability is absolutely essential. They know that if they cannot find God within the confines of the solitude of their own hearts, within their very selves, they cannot find him anywhere. They believe the gospel teaching that says, "The kingdom of God is within you." Under the guidance of the Holy Spirit, they pursue an inner life with God that is truly free, reasonable, and self-directed; controlling their thoughts and passions, watching continuously over the dispositions of their hearts.

For Abba Moses, as with the other abbas, the desire to leave one's solitude and seek distractions, even if they were of a spiritual nature, was a true temptation. This is why when the disciple comes to him asking for a word of wisdom, the old abba promptly sees the disciple's inquiry as an excuse for leaving his cell and thus reprimands him. The disciple is told to give up the illusion of finding wisdom on the outside and to return to his cell and stay there, for "your cell will teach you everything."

Stability and perseverance in one's cell, in spite of the daily temptation brought by boredom, was essential to the life of the desert monk. It was there (and no place else) that he was able to do battle with himself, his passions, and the forces of evil. It was also there that he would come to the true discovery of himself and learn to renounce the false illusions of his older self. In his desert cell, he would patiently learn to renounce one of our supreme worldly values—mobility. But in renouncing it for the sake of God, and by humble perseverance in his seclusion, he would one day obtain from the Lord the gift of peace and inner freedom.

We may not all be able to retire to the seclusion of the desert as the early Fathers did, or even be called to the solitary cell of a monastery, but with the grace of God, we can let go of the many temptations which encumber our spiritual lives. Once we let go of them all, we can then let God into our innermost being. We can establish stability in the solitude of our hearts, and with the aid of the Holy Spirit, preserve the advice of another wise Abba: "Sit in your cell and always be mindful of God."

ABBA JOHN THE DWARF

CHAPTER 4

Essential Monastic Values

Living Faith

Amen, I say to you, if you have faith the size of a mustard seed, you will say to this mountain, 'Move from here to there,' and it will move. Nothing will be impossible for you."

MATTHEW 17:20

Faith is the point of departure when one embarks upon the adventure of the monastic life. Faith, according to the gospels, is the one requirement Jesus makes of his disciples in order that they accomplish God's actions in their midst. It is a very uplifting joy to read the many gospel passages where Jesus attributes the performance of God's wonders to the faith of those who ask for it. To mention just a few, there are the stories of the paralytic lowered through the roof (Luke 5:17–26), the cure of the woman with a hemorrhage and the daughter of Jairus raised to life (Mark 15:21–42), and the healing of the daughter of the Canaanite woman (Matthew 14:21–28). It is also worthwhile to give serious consideration to the rebukes Jesus makes to those of little or no faith and how this lack of faith on our part impedes the accomplishment of God's work in us. See the account of the calming of the storm (Mark 4:35–41), the parable of the unscrupulous judge and the importunate widow (Luke 18:1–8), and the cursing of the barren fig tree (Matthew 21:18–22).

But what is faith? The *Catechism of the Catholic Church* defines it as "the submission of our intellect and our will to God." It is our human response to the God who reveals himself to us and calls us to fellowship with him. What Saint Paul calls "the obedience of faith" (Romans 1:5), according to the catechism, means "to submit freely to the word that has been heard, because its truth is guaranteed by God, who is truth itself."

Faith ultimately is a gift from God—a gift that allows us to place our intellect, our knowledge, ourselves, and our entire lives into the hands of God—the sole reason for our being and living. The moment the gift of faith is bestowed upon us, it changes our life dramatically. It makes all the difference in the world. Faith remains a great mystery, a mystery that seems easier to be experienced by the believer than to be explained to one who has no faith. Through the reality of faith, Christ becomes present in our lives. Through the experience of faith, we sense the power of the Holy Spirit at work in us, changing those things in our lives that are not pleasing to God, and transforming

us more and more into the image of Jesus, the Father's beloved Son.

The catechism proposes Mary, the Mother of God, as a living example of what "obedience of faith" means. Only by appreciating the mystery of her faith can we understand Mary's acceptance of the archangel Gabriel's message and her complete submission to God's will. Deep in her heart she believed that "nothing will be impossible to God" (Luke 1:37), and she gave her assent, which forever changed the course of history. The great mystery of the Incarnation was accomplished in a humble handmaid, whose faith and humility captivated the heart of God himself. Because of her deep faith in God's promises, we Christians of every generation honor her and call her blessed.

Faith is truly a mysterious thing, and we have the freedom to accept or reject it. Mary's faith accepted joyfully the good tidings of the annunciation. This same faith that allowed her to trust God for who he is, however, made her also accept his will during the pains of the crucifixion, when much was asked of her Son and of her, as well, standing at the foot of the cross. She did not understand it all, but she never questioned God, and she knew that in receiving and accepting the gift of faith, there could also be a price to pay.

Doubts may assail us from time to time, as they did, for example, the saints. Saint Thérèse of Lisieux, a nineteenth-century Carmelite nun, suffered enormous doubts and temptations against faith on her deathbed. Though utterly frustrated in a human way, she had complete trust in the word of the Lord and accepted what it had in store for her. Likewise, in our inner journey, we must not succumb in our dark hours of doubt and contradictions, but press on, with our faith firmly grounded in the promise of God's word. There alone lies the solution.

God gives us this life on earth so that we may learn to believe, learn to believe him and his only Son, Jesus, whom he sent into this world to save us. Everything that happens in our daily lives should make us grow deeper and lead us further into this belief. Whatever our problems and struggles, whatever fears and limitations we face daily, through the eyes of faith we shall be able to sense the saving power of God at work in our lives. Faith will show us that our sinfulness, our poverty, and our powerlessness are not obstacles to the workings of God's grace in us. Neither darkness nor terror can overtake us, for we shall be illuminated by the truth and the vision of God, which is incompatible with all darkness.

What treasures of peace, love, and wisdom
You store up, O Lord, for those who believe in you.
You fill them with trust and confidence,
And you shelter them under the shadow of your wings.
Be merciful, to us, O Lord,
And grant us also the same faith,
That we may know the true joy of knowing you
And your only begotten Son, whom you sent to us,
Our Lord Jesus Christ.

Humility

Just as one cannot build a ship unless one has some nails, so it is impossible to be saved without humility.

AMMA SYNCLETICA, *THE SAYINGS OF THE DESERT FATHERS*

It is no great thing to be with God in your thoughts, but it is a great thing to see yourself as inferior to all creatures. It is this, coupled with hard work, that leads to humility.

ABBA SISOES, *THE SAYINGS OF THE DESERT FATHERS*

"*You* have been told, O mortal, what is good, and what the LORD requires of you: Only to do justice and to love goodness, and to walk humbly with your God" (Micah 6:8). This text from an Old Testament prophet sums up Saint Benedict's teaching on humility and could be proposed to all monks as the program of their monastic life. If Saint Benedict places such emphasis on the role of humility in the monks' lives, it is because the gospels themselves teach and require it of all Christians. Humility of spirit is an essential attitude that Jesus demands from all his followers. Even when we perform good deeds, the gospel bids us to remember that we are nothing but "useless servants."

The emphasis on humility in monastic life is one of those aspects that make monasticism so countercultural. Our present-day culture fosters self-assertion, self-exaltation, self-pride, and ultimately self-glorification. The glory is no longer given to God but to the self. The need for humility is replaced by the sin of pride.

In contrast, Jesus teaches in the story of the publican and the Pharisee (Luke 18:9–14) that God wants and expects the total opposite from the Christian. The gospel portrays the Pharisee as self-righteous, arrogant, and proud of himself. In his prayer, he gives a long speech to God, telling him of his accomplishments. The poor publican, however, humbles himself, and his humility pleases the Lord; thus, God hears his humble prayer. The Christian is called to choose the way of the publican. It is only through true humility of heart that the monk can be liberated from the prison of his hopeless self-centeredness.

In making his attitude that of the publican, the monk is imitating the example of Christ himself, who said to all his disciples, "Learn from me, for I am meek and humble of heart" (Matthew 11:29). From the moment of his Incarnation until the end of his life, Jesus humbled himself and became obedient even unto death (Philippians 2:7–8). Jesus is both the teacher and the model for the monk. The monk can measure the validity of his life only by how close he follows the example of the master. The monk then will hear Jesus' consoling promise to those who follow the path of humility: "You will find rest for your souls." This peace of the soul is ultimately the fruit and reward that humility brings to the monk's heart.

The man who had come to know himself is never fooled into reaching for what is beyond him. He keeps his feet henceforth on the blessed path of humility.

Saint John Climacus, *The Ladder of Divine Ascent*

The First Step of Humility

"The first degree of humility, then, is that a man always have the fear of God before his eyes, shunning all forgetfulness and that he be ever mindful of all that God hath commanded, that he always considereth in his mind how those who despise God will burn in hell for their sins, and that life everlasting is prepared for those who fear God. And whilst he guardeth himself evermore against sin and vices of thought, word, deed, and self-will, let him also hasten to cut off the desires of the flesh."

RULE OF SAINT BENEDICT, CHAPTER 7

Saint Benedict took Lent so seriously that he dedicated an entire chapter of the Rule to the subject. He declared in no uncertain terms, "the life of a monk ought to have always the character of a Lenten observance." For Saint Benedict, Lent is not just another

liturgical season among others. Rather, Lent is the season that mirrors most exactly what the life of the monk should be at all times.

Keeping Saint Benedict's views on Lent in mind, I decided a few years ago to concentrate my Lenten meditations on what Saint Benedict wrote in chapter 7 of the Rule. The following comments are an exposé of those early reflections. It goes without saying that the chapter in the Rule dedicated entirely to humility is most obviously connected to the attitude of spirit we must seek to cultivate during Lent.

Humility's first step, as enunciated by Saint Benedict, seems clear and evident. It is a basic principle of all spiritual life. The fear of the Lord is the beginning of wisdom, according to Scriptures. It is also one of the seven gifts of the Holy Spirit. According to Saint Benedict, it makes us realize that God knows each of us through and through and that nothing escapes from his eyes. To him, we are an open book; he can read every word, every line, every sentence. Humility's first step teaches us how to live in God's holy presence: in the spirit of humble repentance for our shortcomings and daily weaknesses, and in the spirit of gratitude for God's infinite patience with each of us.

The Second Step of Humility

The second degree of humility is, when a man loveth not his own will, nor is pleased to fulfill his own desires but by his deeds carrieth out that word of the Lord which saith: "I came not to do My own will but the will of Him that sent Me" (John 6:38). It is likewise said: "Self-will hath its punishment, but necessity winneth the crown."

RULE OF SAINT BENEDICT, CHAPTER 7

The essence of the Christian life is the imitation of the life of Christ. He is the only model. He is also the master and we are the disciples. The master utters the invitation: "Whoever wishes to come after me must deny himself, take up his cross, and follow me." In order to follow Jesus, we must embrace the cross, the small crosses of everyday life, and follow the path of self-renunciation. This is not easy, for we know it to be so contrary to human nature.

Jesus never promised us that the way to heaven would be an easy one. What he promised was to send us a comforter who would remind us of Jesus' teachings and words and at the same time give us the strength and necessary fortitude to follow the ways of the gospel, no matter how perilous they may seem to be.

In the Our Father we pray daily, "thy will be done on earth as it is in heaven." This is precisely what Saint Benedict encourages us to seek through the practice of humility's second step: acceptance of the will of God in our daily life and in all of our actions. In accomplishing the will of the Father, we shall discover our true freedom, our only joy, and our perfect peace.

The Third Step of Humility

The third degree of humility is, that for the love of God a man subject himself to a Superior in all obedience, imitating the Lord, of whom the Apostle saith: "He became obedient unto death" (Philippians 2:8).

RULE OF SAINT BENEDICT, CHAPTER 7

The mystery of monastic obedience, and its only justification, is based on Jesus' attitude toward his heavenly Father. Jesus' entrance into the world was marked by the words: "Behold, I come to do thy will." Throughout his thirty-three years on earth, he not only obeyed his heavenly Father, but also his Mother Mary and his stepfather Joseph. This submission to his Father was carried out to the end of his life, obediently accepting even death—on a cross!

Following the example of Christ, the monk promises to remain obedient "even unto death" in the monastery of his profession. This monastic obedience is manifested by humble fidelity and daily submission to the will of God, to the Church (which is Christ's body), to the Rule, to the monastic tradition, to the Father of the community, and to one another. Obedience allows the monk to become a servant as Christ became one for our sake. Obedience, for the monk, is expressed ultimately in the humble respect he shows toward the superior, his brothers in the monastery, and all those he comes in contact with in daily life, seeing Christ in all of them.

The Fourth Step of Humility

The fourth degree of humility is, that, if hard and distasteful things are commanded, nay, even though injuries are inflicted, he accept them with patience and even temper, and not grow weary or give up.

RULE OF SAINT BENEDICT, CHAPTER 7

The practice of the fourth step of humility, according to Saint Benedict, is very demanding and at times painful. It is only in light of the mystery of the cross of Christ and of his supreme obedience to the Father that we can begin to apprehend the hardship entailed in this form of following the Lord. When we think physical suffering is difficult to endure, we soon find out that mental and emotional suffering is much more painful. Only those who have endured unjust persecution and the mental anguish that this sort of suffering carries with it have experiential knowledge of how painful it is to assent to God's will under such circumstances.

It's not surprising, then, if in a moment of weakness or fear we try to escape from it. Jesus himself prayed to the Father: "Father, if it is possible, let this cup pass from me." It is only human to wish to escape unhurt. But it is precisely at this moment, "with a quiet heart," as counseled by Saint Benedict, that we try to submit to God's wishes as we utter the remainder of Jesus' words: "Yet, not as I will, but as you will." In this submission, we shall begin to feel that all natural resentment emanating from the source of this suffering begins to lessen, and a deep inner peace settles in. That peace is a sure sign of the healing presence of God within us.

The Fifth Step of Humility

The fifth degree of humility is, when one hideth from his Abbot none of the evil thoughts which rise in his heart or the evils committed by him in secret, but humbly confesseth them. Concerning this the Scripture exhorts us, saying: "Make known your way to the Lord, and hope in him" (Psalm 36).

RULE OF SAINT BENEDICT, CHAPTER 7

*I*t has always been a part of the monastic tradition that the young monk who enters a monastery is put under the care of a spiritual father, either the abbot himself or another older spiritual teacher. It is the purpose of the spiritual father to form, direct, and transmit to the new novice the principles of the monastic life. Furthermore, the spiritual father has the delicate task of helping to generate the inner life of the neophyte monk. This implies great trust on the part of both the spiritual father and the spiritual son. But it is impossible, in the eyes of Saint Benedict, to arrive to this level of profound mutual trust without first acquiring great humility of heart. The novice must look at the spiritual father as someone standing in the Lord's place and open the innermost sentiments of his heart. A wise spiritual father is there to engender the life of the Spirit in his spiritual son. The spiritual son, with a humble attitude and without fear, can communicate to the father all that is within him, no matter how wicked or sinful it may seem. This is absolutely necessary if the new young monk is going to make any progress in the spiritual life.

What Saint Benedict proposed to the new aspirant to the monastic life is applicable not only to monks and nuns, but also to all who wish to grow in their spiritual life. We all need to open ourselves with sincere humility, either to a spiritual father or mother or to a confessor or a director, in order to be shown the light and the path that we must follow. The result of doing this will be manifested in the strengthening of the spiritual life and the deep peace acquired by the person receiving the direction.

The Sixth Step of Humility

The sixth degree of humility is, when a monk is content with the meanest and worst of everything, and in all that is enjoined him holdeth himself as a bad and worthless workman.

RULE OF SAINT BENEDICT, CHAPTER 7

Saint Benedict, heeding the words of the gospels, knew the dangers of self-aggrandizement, a temptation so common among people who make a claim of being spiritual. And there are plenty of them today. But in the words of Jesus, we must always seek the last place and make ourselves the servant of all.

The servant is not greater than the master, says the Lord, and if he chose to empty himself by taking the form of a servant, it was to give us an example of how we must follow him. To choose therefore the lowest and the last place in all circumstances, to acknowledge oneself as the "useless servant" even when we think we have achieved some good, are the genuine signs of true discipleship. The Lord rewards the humility of the servant by granting him or her true inner freedom. For in truth, one need not do battle or compete for the last place, since very few aspire to such a position. In choosing to always be last, we choose to be let alone with God, in a place where no one is allowed to disturb this intimate communion.

The Seventh Step of Humility

The seventh degree of humility is, when, not only with his tongue he declareth, but also in his inmost soul believeth, that he is the lowest and vilest of men, humbling himself and saying with the Prophet: "I am truly a worm, not a man, scorned by men and despised by the people..." And again, "It is a blessing that you have humbled me so that I can learn your commandment."

RULE OF SAINT BENEDICT, CHAPTER 7

Saint Benedict attaches such importance to humility in the spiritual life that he writes about it in the Rule in one of its incipient chapters, right after the chapters on obedience and on restraint of speech. He knows that it is impossible to advance in any spiritual life without being rooted in the solid foundations of humility. Through the years I have learned again and again to recognize someone as truly spiritual not by their outer gifts and talents but by their profound humility: the type of humility where little is left of the self and only the light of God shines through the person. When one is given the grace to encounter such individuals (and they are indeed very rare, very few) one is left with a profound sense of the presence of God. As our Lord tells us clearly in the gospels: by their fruits you shall recognize them. When one is fortunate to meet one of them, I find them to be the most attractive human beings on earth, the most authentically human, the most full of God.

In the seventh step of humility, Saint Benedict invites us to go one step deeper into the practice of true humility, not just paying lip service to it, but admitting to ourselves our misery and nothingness, the fact that we are useless servants of no value at all. Saint Benedict invites us to rejoice in this fact and encourages us to wish that others will see us as such, and not as something we are not. It is when we become nothing in our own eyes and in the eyes of others that God turns himself toward us in mercy and finds his true pleasure in us.

In the Magnificat, which we sing daily at vespers, our Lady affirms without any doubt this spiritual truth: Because he has looked with favor on the lowliness of her servant, therefore the Almighty has done great things for me. And a bit later she adds: He has scattered the proud in their conceit, he has cast down the mighty from their thrones, and he has lifted up the lowly. If we are indeed serious about pleasing God, about becoming his instruments, we must strive always for the last place in all things: what Charles de Foucauld would call the "dear last place."

The Eighth Step of Humility

The eighth degree of humility is, when a monk doeth nothing but what is sanctioned by the common rule of the monastery and the example of his elders.

RULE OF SAINT BENEDICT, CHAPTER 7

*J*f I chose Saint Benedict's chapter on humility as the point of our Lenten meditations, it is simply because I realize that no true spiritual progress or true repentance can take place without embracing the path of humility and all it entails. There is no way of avoiding it. Our Lord insists: Learn from me, for I am meek and humble of heart.

The eighth degree of humility is a very subtle one. It has both individual and communal implications. The temptation to think that we, individuals or as a community, are better than others is a subtle but very real one. In our days we see it expressed all around us in one form or another. How many monasteries and communities succumb to the temptation that they are the only true faithful heirs to the ideals of their founders, as if others were not? Sometimes they go so far as to call themselves "the Reform of the reform." Well-intentioned as they may be, I can't help but detect how pride creeps in even in good, well-intentioned people. There are others who refuse to accept the liturgical reform approved by the Vatican Council, implying they know better than the Holy Spirit, and say that their role is to save the Church from peril. I have sometimes witnessed this in France, and without passing judgment on particular individuals or communities, I couldn't help but notice how the demon uses pride in a subtle way to infiltrate his ideas into those who honestly try to serve God. At times I have heard monks state *Nous sommes des pilliers de l'Eglise*, or, "We are the true pillars of the Church." In repeating this to a very holy and old monk who has since died, remarkable for his wisdom as for his humility, he replied, "Son, when we monks start thinking like that, the best thing for us is to die and disappear. We are of no use to the Lord. The glory we should ascribe to him alone, we ascribe to ourselves."

Pride and self-love are such strong powers in all of us that Saint Francis of Sales indicates they die in us only fifteen minutes after our own death. When Saint Benedict admonishes us to find our place within the common rule of the monastery or the society we live in, so as not to be distinguished from others, he is simply trying to remind us of the constant danger and temptation of pride, where we seek to be exalted above others. At a given time, when we are persecuted and real humiliations descend upon us, we must see them as grace, as real signs of how much God cares for us. This may be a hard lesson to learn. As Jesus mentions in the gospels, some of his teachings are hard to accept, but at the end there is no choice. Either we choose the path of self-glorification that has no future and dies, or we choose the path of God that leads to true life.

The Ninth Step of Humility

The ninth degree of humility is, when a monk withholdeth his tongue from speaking, and keeping silence doth not speak until he is asked; for the Scripture showeth that "in a flood of words you will not avoid sinning," and "a talkative man goes about aimlessly on earth."

RULE OF SAINT BENEDICT, CHAPTER 7

*A*ccording to Saint Benedict and the ancient monastic fathers, silence and a certain amount of solitude are indispensable if one is to pursue an authentic spiritual life. Already in the Old Testament we hear the Lord saying to the prophet Hosea: "I will allure her now; I will lead her into the wilderness and speak persuasively to her." The voice of God can almost never be heard, except in deep silence and profound solitude.

If Saint Benedict insists on the practice of silence as a means of achieving true humility, it is simply because he knows human nature. He knows the proud man loves to assert himself, loves to hear himself speaking. How often we find ourselves in the middle of a conversation, anxious for the other person to end a sentence so that we can interject our own opinion. We sometimes don't even bother listening to what the other has to say. All we wish is to make ourselves heard. It is against such human temptations as pride, self-assertion, self-preference, and self-opinion that Saint Benedict counsels control over our tongues through the practice of silence. This is indispensable for true communion with God. Another great desert figure, Saint John the Baptist, notes that the decreasing of the self in us is directly proportional to the increasing of the life of God within us. This is the wisdom and eternal paradox of the gospels, authenticated throughout the ages by the example of the saints.

The Tenth Step of Humility

The tenth degree of humility is, when a monk is not easily moved and quick for laughter, for it is written: "Only a fool raises his voice in laughter."
RULE OF SAINT BENEDICT, CHAPTER 7

$\mathcal{R}$ eaders who are not well-acquainted with the monastic tradition may be a bit surprised at what Saint Benedict is referring to here. It is not an easy part of the Rule to interpret. As a matter of fact, one commentator on the Rule says, "Since it is a short expose, the commentary should likewise be short." This being said, as a longtime student of the Rule, I can't help but try to read some meaning into it. Especially since I know well that Saint Benedict is rather frugal and never wasteful in his use of words.

The first thing that comes to mind is that Saint Benedict, human as he was and always striving for moderation in all things, is not totally opposed to laughter; only to certain types of laughter that are not becoming of a spiritual person. Take, for example, a sarcastic type of laughter that implies a certain arrogance toward a neighbor; or the frivolous laughter that makes mockery of everything, and which, again, is not only a sign of intemperance but also of pride. And certainly, it seems perfectly natural that a loud laughter would be considered totally unbecoming to a quiet, recollected spirit.

If the spiritual person is discouraged from exercising this sort of laughter by Saint Benedict, he says nothing whatsoever about forbidding a beautiful smile on the monk, which may reflect the peace and the joy of his union with God. A peaceful and radiant smile can do so much to reflect the presence of God in oneself. I think of Jesus' apparition to his disciples after the resurrection. I am sure he smiled beautifully and serenely when he greeted them with his "Peace be with you." And in many apparitions of our Lady, such as the one at Lourdes, Bernadette often referred to her beautiful and tender smile. While a loud laugh may be considered a sign of pride and incongruous to the monastic life according to Saint Benedict, he never discourages the monk from radiating a humble, peaceful, and benevolent smile. This type of smile may go a long way in influencing others to glorify God in all things.

The Eleventh Step of Humility

The eleventh degree of humility is, that, when a monk speaketh, he speak gently and without laughter, humbly and with gravity, with few and sensible words, and that he be not loud of voice, as it is written: "A wise man is known by his few words."

RULE OF SAINT BENEDICT, CHAPTER 7

For Saint Benedict, there is an inner logic in the ladder of ascent toward attaining true humility. All the steps are connected in the one ladder. And so it seems that the eleventh step is a natural prolongation of the tenth step, while adding a new element to it. Saint Benedict, in this passage, not only mentions to avoid laughter; he goes further and counsels the monk to speak gently, briefly, with few words, and always with sincere modesty.

Saint Benedict is not only concerned with the inner workings of the monk, but also with his external behavior, which often becomes a reflection of his inner state. In the spiritual life, our interior and external conduct are intimately connected. They can never be separated. Saint Paul, in his Letter to the Galatians, expands for us Saint Benedict's exhortation on humility's eleventh step. Let me put it like this: If you are guided by the Spirit you will be in no danger of yielding to self-indulgence, since self-indulgence is the opposite of the Spirit. What the Spirit brings is very different: love, joy, peace, patience, goodness, trustfulness, gentleness, and self-control. There can be no law against things like that, of course. You cannot belong to Christ Jesus unless you crucify all self-indulgent passions and desires. Since the Spirit is our life, let us be directed by the Spirit. We must stop being conceited, provocative and envious (Galatians 5:16–26).

The Twelfth Step of Humility

The twelfth degree of humility is, when a monk is not only humble of heart, but always letteth it appear also in his whole exterior to all that see him; namely, at the Work of God, in the garden, on a journey, in the field, or wherever he may be, sitting, walking, or standing, let him always have his head bowed down, his eyes fixed on the ground, ever holding himself guilty of his sins, thinking that he is already standing before the dread judgment seat of God, and always saying to himself in his heart what the publican in the Gospel said, with his eyes fixed on the ground: "Lord, I am a sinner, not worthy to look up to heaven." And with the Prophet: "I am bowed down and humbled in every way."

Rule of Saint Benedict, chapter 7

During our pilgrimage toward the pasch, Saint Benedict, with his usual wisdom, keeps reminding us that our monastic lives must reflect a Lenten character at all times, not solely during Lent. Coincidentally, in one of the gospel readings the Church presents for our consideration during Lent, the story of the Pharisee and the Publican in Luke 18:9–14 to which Saint Benedict makes reference to the twelfth step for attaining humility. The temptation to pride, to self-exaltation, to being conceited, to thinking oneself better than others remains with us until the end of our days. All we can do is face the war within ourselves, as did the ancient Desert Fathers and Mothers. The weapon they used in the battle was the continual recitation, day and night, of the Publican's prayer: "God, be merciful to me a sinner."

Throughout the centuries the formula of that prayer developed into what has become now the Jesus prayer: "Lord Jesus Christ, Son of the living God, have mercy on me a sinner." The Jesus prayer allows us to confront ourselves daily, as in a mirror. We look at ourselves and all we see is the naked truth about our crude sinfulness, our failings, our shortcomings, our pride, our lack of charity, or our passing judgment on others. In the Jesus prayer there is no escape from this sort of harsh self-confrontation. The only way out of it is the true recognition of our sinful state and the knowledge of the abundant mercy waiting to those who humble themselves. There is a river of love and mercy, with a flow of profound peace, for all those who, in the words of Saint Benedict, "constantly say in his heart what the Publican said in the gospel." For the time comes, after years of faithful praying, when by the grace of God the prayer takes hold of one's being and becomes one with us. Then, no obstacles remain between the humble realization of our sinfulness and the gift of forgiveness received from a loving Father. When that moment arrives, we are reminded of the words of Jesus: There is more rejoicing in heaven over one repentant sinner than over ninety-nine virtuous men who have no need of repentance.

While writing about this twelfth step, Saint Benedict approaches also the physical conduct and the bearing the monk must have at all times, whether he sits, walks or stands, or whether he is in the oratory or garden, on a journey or in the field, or anywhere else. We are both body and soul, and our physical bearing ought to be a reflection of our inner dispositions. This sort of behavior or comportment on the part of the monk is what the ancient fathers taught as monastic modesty. Modesty is the opposite of pride, the monk's great enemy. And by holding on in all things to the habitual practice of monastic modesty on a daily basis, little by little we let go of the false self. We die daily, to make room for God. We let go of ourselves, and in doing that we let God in.

Silence

Silence is the mystery of the world to come,
Speech is the organ of this present world....
Every man who so delights in a multitude of words,
Even if he says admirable things, is empty within.
Silence, however, will illuminate you in God
And deliver you from the phantoms of ignorance.
      SAINT ISAAC OF NINEVAH

ilence is a very important aspect of all traditional monastic life. For the monk, silence creates a space where the integration of his scattered powers into a unity becomes possible. The silence of the monastery cultivates a necessary ambiance where the monk can come to the knowledge and experience of God and can better apprehend the mystery of his love. Silence purifies love in our hearts and strengthens and deepens our prayer. It brings light and clarity to the darkness of our minds; it gives peace and endurance to our daily work. Silence is the source of strength, harmony, and stability in the monastic day.

Exterior and interior silence is essential to the monastic life. The very nature of our style of life demands an attitude of reverence for silence. Situated in a secluded area, the monastery provides the tranquility necessary for the development of the monk's interior life.

Saint Benedict's Rule quotes Old Testament passages where the abuse of speech—too much talking—leads to sin, and he strongly recommends that it be curbed. Saint Benedict goes beyond the simple use of silence as a repressive measure to avoid sin. He sees silence as a liberating force that frees the monk's soul to raise itself to God. In the monk who loves silence, the working of grace is given greater freedom.

Silence is observed in monasteries in a variety of forms. There may be some insignificant differences between individual monasteries in the way silence is kept, but the essential respect for it permeates every contemplative monastery where the Rule is taken seriously. In every monastery there are "spaces of silence," where speech or conversation is not allowed. These are usually the oratory, the refectory, the dormitory and cells, the cloister, the library, and the scriptorium. The monk is taught from his very entrance into monastic life to be deferential toward the silence of others. Because of this, silence is required in all the places where the life of the community unfolds. Silence is also observed in a stricter fashion at certain times of the day: during the night (called in monasteries "the great silence," from compline to after the completion of the morning Office), during the siesta in summer, during the hours of prayer and *lectio*, and during the meals, when reading accompanies the partaking of food.

The habit of silence among monks does not apply only to speech or conversation. Monks are encouraged to practice quiet in many practical ways, such as avoiding making noise when they walk, sit, work, close or open a door or a window. When speaking is necessary and conversations take place, monks are still quiet, subdued, and restrained—as Saint Benedict suggests.

To the extent that the monk is serious about the cultivation of silence, either in the hermitage or the monastery, the more he is filled with the tranquility, peace, and necessary grace to apprehend the presence of God in the depths of his soul.

These three things are appropriate for a monk: exile, poverty, and endurance in silence.

ABBA ANDREW, *THE SAYINGS OF THE DESERT FATHERS*

Solitude

Solitude and prayer are the greatest means to acquire virtues. Purifying the mind, they make it possible to see the unseen.

Solitude, prayer, love, and abstinence are the four wheels of the vehicle that carries our spirit heavenward.

SAINT SERAPHIM OF SAROV

Solitude is an inner journey which monks, and all men and women alike, who seek the truth must make at one time, or preferably frequently, during their earthly lives. The difference between those who embrace the monastic state and those who don't is that we monks not only accept the necessity and the validity of this journey, but we also encourage it and make time for it.

The journey into solitude fosters a quest for our true self; not

the person that we and others think we are, but the person that God expects us to be, made as we are in his image and likeness. Of course, this is a lifelong journey, not accomplished all at once but requiring frequent and perhaps long sojourns into solitude. Solitude helps us face the fact that we are all, monks included, victims of the pretensions, vanity, and illusions of a worldly society that nurtures in us a false portrait of the self and not the true self that God intends. Solitude is the place where we find the grace to face the struggle between these two selves, the false one and the true one. Solitude is also where we encounter a God who loves us, a God who is love, life, mercy, light, and truth and who leads us gently on the path to the discovery of our true identity. Solitude is the place where the old fractured self dies and the new transformed self, helped by God's grace, emerges.

Thomas Merton, the renowned Cistercian monk and a lover of solitude, expanded on this search for the authentic self in many of his treatises. In "The Inner Experience: Christian Contemplation," he once poignantly wrote:

I must return to Paradise.
I must recover myself,
salvage my dignity,
recollect my lost wits,
return to my true identity.

The early desert monks, with that deep realism and profound common sense that was uniquely theirs, also taught their disciples to cultivate the love of solitude. Again and again they repeated, "Stay in your cell and do not leave it. Sit in your cell, and your cell will teach you everything." For them, the humble solitude of the monastic cell was the furnace of Babylon, where the transformation from the old self into the new self in God's likeness took place. The task of the disciple was to heed his master's advice and persevere, in spite of the trials and often boredom of the cell, along with him who is alone. Gradually the disciple learned to discover the wisdom of this teaching. Solitude then became for him not only the place that led to the discovery of his true identity, but it even more so became the place where he could find and work out daily his own salvation.

In the swamp in secluded recesses,
A shy and hidden bird is warbling a song.
Solitary the thrush,
The hermit withdrawn to himself, avoiding the settlements,
Sings by himself a song.
    WALT WHITMAN, FROM *WHEN LILACS LAST IN THE DOORYARD BLOOM'D*

Purity of Heart

Let us aim at our principal goal, at that purity of heart which is love.
Saint John Cassian, Conferences 1

With all vigilance guard your heart,
for in it are the sources of life.
Proverbs 4:23

According to the teachings of Saint John Cassian, one of the early monastic fathers, the primary aim of the monastic journey is to work to achieve the "purity of heart" to which the gospel promise is attached: "Blessed are the clean of heart, for they shall see God" (Matthew 5:8). Of course, this is not an easy or short-term task for the monk. It demands humility, renunciation, constant vigilance, unceasing prayer, and most of all, grace from the Holy Spirit. Purity of heart is not achieved in a single day, month, or year. It is rather the result of a long, slow process, a process sometimes tedious and cumbersome, by which the monk learns to die daily so that he may live in God alone.

Purity of heart allows the monk to return to the center of his being, where God dwells and where he is most himself. In that center, all things converge and come together. The gospel never ceases to remind us that "the kingdom of God is within us," and not anywhere else. To lose sight of that unique and precious center is to diminish our capacity for the genuine purity of heart required for the vision of God. During our earthly journey, our constant petition to the Holy Spirit must be to enable us to travel ever deeper into that center where he is our most delightful guest. It is there, according to Jesus' promises, that the Spirit will teach us all things. Through the power of the Holy Spirit, the true dynamic force in the life of the Christian, we shall be able to slowly make progress into the ways of love and eventually arrive to the final vision of he who is love itself.

Simplicity

If you wish to draw the Lord to you, approach him as disciples to a master, in all simplicity, openly, honestly, without duplicity, without idle curiosity. God is simple and uncompounded, and he wants the souls that come to him to be simple and pure. Indeed, you will never see simplicity separated from humility.

SAINT JOHN CLIMACUS, *THE LADDER OF DIVINE ASCENT*

True simplicity consists not in the use of particular forms, but in foregoing overindulgence, in maintaining humility of spirit, and in keeping the material surroundings of our lives directly serviceable to necessary ends, even though these surroundings may properly be characterized by grace, symmetry, and beauty.

BOOK OF DISCIPLINE OF THE RELIGIOUS SOCIETY OF FRIENDS

*P*art of the gospel message, exemplified in the life of Jesus, is an invitation to the Christian to choose true simplicity of heart, of mind, of lifestyle. Jesus was born, lived, and died in great simplicity, and the task of the disciple is to follow in the footsteps of the master—for the disciple is no greater than the master (Matthew 10:24). As a matter of fact, true acceptance of the gospel, as we witness in the lives of the saints, implies a simplified and unified existence. Christian life is truly a call to radical simplicity.

From our daily experiences, we learn that human existence is complex. We are attracted to many things at the same time, and our lives bear witness to diverse cultural, spiritual, and biological factors. We see nations at war with one another; we see ourselves as human beings at odds with one another. We feel the conflict between the body and the spirit, the tension between the mind and the heart, the rift between the individual and society at large, the strife between humankind and our environment. Complexity exists at the very core of our human existence, it is a daily fact of life, and we are often unable to handle its weight, tensions, and seeds of destruction.

How does the Christian monastic react to all of this? Where does he or she look for enlightenment and resolution to seemingly unsolvable tensions? The answer can only lie in the acceptance of the gospel and its fundamental message of simplicity, based on the life and teachings of Jesus, who is the foundation rock of our faith.

As Christians, monks, and nuns, we strive for the single-mindedness of the gospel (or what may be called simplicity of the intellect) through the complete surrender of our minds to truth.

 But first, filled with deep humility, we must readily acknowledge and accept the limitations of our minds and renounce all our intellectual self-presumptions and illusions. There is nothing more dangerous in a spiritual life than an attitude of vanity, superiority, and self-importance, which manifests itself in many subtle ways. Once we have renounced our self-interest and acknowledged our capacity to know and understand nothing, it is only then that our minds, enlightened by the Holy Spirit, become capable of the clear pursuit of truth for its own sake. In the process, we are given the grace to discover that truth itself is a person, for the Lord says, "I am...the truth" (John 14:6). He prays to the Father to be rooted and consecrated in this truth (John 17:19). Grasping

this truth is ever beyond the normal comprehension of our limited human minds. But God allows those who seek him with simplicity of mind and purity of heart to discover and hold onto him who alone is truth and who designs to show us, in his mercy, the path to life.

Authentic simplicity of heart means essentially the continual practice of self-renunciation in every life situation and turning from every form of worldly illusion. It is certainly the antithesis to the ways and wisdom of the world. "True simplicity," as the Shakers liked to call it, or "blessed simplicity," as the early Christian monks called it, helps to liberate our hearts from the worship of false idols and the exaggerated self-exaltation and glorification that is so in vogue in our day, even among so-called spiritual people. Instead, real simplicity of heart fosters within us an indescribable longing for God and his kingdom. Seek first the kingdom of God (Matthew 6:33), Jesus tells us, and this we do by giving ourselves to the task of unceasing prayer (Luke 21:36). This, in turn, allows us to experience the groaning of the Holy Spirit within the enclosure of our hearts, that is, at the very root of our being. This is the fulfillment of the Lord's promise when he says in the gospel, "Blessed are the pure in heart, for they shall see God" (Matthew 5:8, *RSV*), for indeed simplicity of heart is nothing else than this purity of heart to which Jesus attaches the beautiful promise of the vision of God.

However, it is not possible to strive for monastic simplicity of mind and heart without also adopting a simple lifestyle. Following the example of the master, monks and nuns seek to do away with all that is inessential in their everyday lives and live with total dependence upon God. The Christian monastic is called to renounce worldly cares and attachments and, with ever-increasing faith and passionate love for the Lord, to surrender completely to God's loving Providence. With childlike simplicity we entrust our lives, our fears, our basic need for security, and everything else to our Father's loving care. Do not "worry about your life, what you will eat [or drink], or about your body, what you will wear....Your heavenly Father knows that you need them all" (Matthew 6:25, 32).

Monastic simplicity, thus understood, becomes a radical reaction to the false stability and security the world offers, a true beacon of hope toward attaining the blessed freedom of God's children. This simplicity directs our hearts and minds—indeed, all of our actions— toward God, in whom alone the resolution and integration of our apparent complexities can be found. Monastic simplicity purifies our hearts, unifies our sense of purpose, and redirects it toward the kingdom of God. Accepted as a way of life, simplicity liberates us not only from the heavy burden of complexities but also frees us from the weight of our attachment to material, temporal things, allowing us to focus single-heartedly on Jesus, our Savior. Monastic simplicity sets us free from the violence and the conflicts found in and outside ourselves, assuring us that a true life in Christ is peace and joy in the Holy Spirit. Finally, true gospel simplicity brings us to the ultimate experience of the transparency of truth; the kind of truth of which Jesus spoke when he said, "I am the way and the truth and the life" (John 14:6).

The older I grow, the more clearly I perceive the dignity and the winning beauty of simplicity in thought, conduct, and speech: a desire to simplify all that is complicated and to treat everything with the greatest naturalness and clarity.

POPE JOHN XXIII

In simplicity, we enter the deep silences of the heart for which we were created.

RICHARD J. FOSTER, *FREEDOM OF SIMPLICTY*

Frugality

A frugal man should always be looking to see what he can do without.
BLESSED HENRY SUSO

Be frugal and hard working men and women; avoid all vanity in dress which will exclude you from heaven; try to keep to the simplicity of manners of our forefathers [and foremothers].
SAINT NICHOLAS OF FLUE, SWISS HERMIT

Frugality and simplicity are cherished virtues within the monastic tradition because they come from the teachings of the gospel and the example of Christ's own life. The first monks and nuns in the desert paid heed to these attractive virtues, leaving us their examples and teachings as testaments.

Through the practice of voluntary frugality we foster a certain attitude in the monastery, a certain philosophy of life that is radically opposed to the values of present-day society. We view the consumerism encouraged by governments, markets, the media, and certain economists as totally unnecessary, wasteful, and certainly harmful to the life of the spirit. The monk's daily life tries to affirm the truth that we can all live better by learning to live with less, and we deliberately assert our inner freedom by renouncing the slavery of overconsumption.

Voluntary frugality doesn't mean necessarily living in a state of destitution. It's a matter of learning to distinguish between the things that we really need in daily life and those that we don't and can do without. It means buying something because it is needed in the monastery, not simply because we want it. It means treating objects, tools, and utensils with such respect that they can last more than a lifetime. It means both refusing to take part in any kind of waste and being thrifty enough to recycle most of the products discarded by our materialistic, wasteful society. Ultimately, frugality is a tool that helps us monks place our values, perspectives, and priorities on what is really important, on the one thing necessary.

When it comes to food, we have a few chickens that provide us with eggs. A garden provides vegetables during the growing season; we freeze and preserve some for the cold months. Besides the food from our gardens, one of the largest food stores in the county gives us a certain amount of vegetables and fruits that they can't sell, some of which we use to feed our animals, some of which we share with those in need, and some of which we eat ourselves. We do the same with the day-old bread and pastries that two local bakeries provide. Sometimes we even get cakes, as we did this past Christmas Eve,

which we were able to serve afterward to all those who came to attend Christmas Mass.

Monastic life has always, like the gospels, been countercultural. While society's incentive is to spend, expand, consume, and waste, monastics choose the opposite as a valid alternative: spend and consume less, scale back on your possessions, avoid cluttering, share and give away to others what you don't need, build small dwellings, and conserve energy and other resources. Monks deliberately make the choice of the good life instead of the trendy fast track of our times.

The frugal life-example of monks has something to offer the world, which is largely directed to the slavery of consumption (often at the expense of the poor and the underprivileged of our planet). The monastic lessons of frugality, austerity, sobriety, and productivity have proven to be a more human, more Christ-like, and a freeing alternative to the seductive, superficial view espoused by a materialistically oriented world.

Let us learn to live simply and frugally,
so that others may simply live.

Inner Freedom

"If you remain in my word,
you will truly be my disciples,
and you will know the truth,
and the truth will set you free."
JOHN 8:31–32

To those who wish to achieve inner freedom, Jesus seems to demand first that they seek the truth of his word, or truth itself, for he says "I am...the truth," (John 14:6). Then this truth will bestow on us the gift of freedom.

In order to become free, however, we must first accept the realization that we are not really free. A humble, honest self-appraisal, a deep look into ourselves, will tell us that we are basically slaves—slaves of our sinfulness, habits, and vices; slaves of our prejudices and intolerance; slaves of our present culture and worldly ideas; slaves of the self-image we have created of ourselves, the idealized self that we portray and wish others to believe is the real us, when in fact it is not. Almost nothing is more difficult than to look at ourselves as we really are. Even more difficult yet is to accept ourselves as God ultimately accepts us. It takes a great deal of courage, humility, and honesty. That in fact is a grace.

It helps to start with the fact that Christ sees us the way we really are yet loves us. He loves us in spite of all our wicked sinfulness, our sometimes ugly behavior, our shortcomings and limitations. If Jesus accepts us and loves us just as we are, then perhaps we can begin accepting ourselves as we are and also begin to love ourselves, in spite of all, for who we indeed are.

The way to inner freedom is the way of humility and truth. We must accept ourselves as we are and others as they are with simplicity, sometimes with humor, and always with love. Love is a sign of God's presence in our lives, and it allows us to reach others beyond the narrow frame of our own selfhood.

Once we love and accept ourselves and do the same with others, we grow into the gift of inner freedom by listening and living out Jesus' gospel words without fear. His words, the truth, will shape every moment of our lives in such a way that we will taste in anticipation something of the joy of heaven, the supreme joy of knowing ourselves to be God's children, totally loved by him.

Lord, Jesus Christ,
You are the way, the truth, and the life.
Lead us through the example
Of your life and the wisdom of your teachings
Into the path of self-discovery
And true acceptance of ourselves
As we really are in your sight.
Help us abide by your word,
The source of all truth,
That in due time we may achieve the inner freedom
Promised to all those who leave all things behind,
And follow you alone until the end.

Serenity

Detach yourself from the love of the multitude, lest your enemy question your spirit and trouble your inner peace.
    ABBA DOUGLAS, *THE SAYINGS OF THE DESERT FATHERS*

Life in our twenty-first century (or the digital age, as many call it) has become the epitome of complexity, noise, consumerism, anxiety, and loneliness. Perhaps one of our most difficult tasks is to cultivate inner peace and serenity, yet all of us deeply yearn for it.

Part of the reason it is hard for us to achieve serenity and inner freedom is that we have become accustomed to living with the false values, rhythms, and images that our present culture promotes. We believe we need them in our lives, when they are totally unnecessary. How can we achieve inner peace when at the same time we long for the company of crowds, are always in a hurry, always have so much to do, are planning endless new things? We thus escape the fact that we don't want to face ourselves being alone. This sort of trend in people's everyday lives is really a sickness, a symptom of something deeply wrong, and the real enemy of serenity.

If we are serious about pursuing peace, one of the first things we need to do is to bring all needless activities to a halt. We need to take time to reflect, pray, and set goals of how to go about changing our lives. A radical change is a must, otherwise nothing will ever be achieved. We need to set our priorities straight and go about organizing a life of simplicity and centeredness, where quiet, prayer, and solitude become the real values. We must recover or discover a real inner rhythm in our lives and feel its liberating pulse.

We must start by first seeking or creating quiet places where we can spend a few hours a day in an ambiance that provides true grounding for the mind and the spirit. In our quest for serenity, it is important to identify, affirm, and support the inner grounding of our being. This can only be done in a space where quiet and solitude are nurtured carefully—hence the value of monasteries and retreat houses that provide this sort of haven in our midst. There it is possible to go and hear the sounds of silence, feel the spaces of solitude, and, ultimately, enter into a state of being that makes a true encounter with God possible, the source of all serenity and peace.

In the solitude and quiet of a monastery, we discover that it is possible to achieve a life made of beauty, harmony, simplicity, and centeredness. We may also discover that it is possible to return to the so-called real world letting go of its glamour, anxiety, clutter, and complexity by choosing to lead a life directed toward communion with God, in whom there is neither anxiety nor complexity, but only peace, love, joy, serenity, and tranquillity. Ultimately, our life's journey becomes what we make of it, and this necessitates a choice.

To you, O God, we turn for peace...
Grant us too the blessed assurance
that nothing shall deprive us of that peace,
neither ourselves,
nor our foolish earthly desires,
nor my wild longings,
nor the anxious cravings of my heart.
Søren Kierkegaard

Obedience

Jesus said: "My food is to do the will of the one who sent me and to finish his work."
JOHN 4:34

The function of faith in obedience is to make the monk see it is God himself whom he obeys each and every time he answers a bell, fulfills a request favor, carries out a wish or command of a superior or anothre brother. Faith keeps the monk sensitive to God's voice speaking through his spokesman.
DOM WILFRED TUNINK, VISION OF PEACE

To obey is to commit oneself to the state of being a servant as Christ was, and thus to make a total offering of oneself.
DOM ANDRE LAUF, THE CISTERCIAN WAY

The monk's obedience is based on Jesus' attitude toward his Father. Jesus' entrance into the world was marked by, "Behold, I come to do thy will," and his daily prayer, "Thy will be done." The monastic concept of obedience is not simply legalistic, but one of complete openness and fidelity to the will of the Father as it reveals itself in the monk's very ordinary daily life. Following the example of the Lord, the monk promises to remain obedient "even unto death" in the monastery. This obedience in monastic life implies fidelity and obedience to the will of God, to the Rule and the monastic tradition, to the father of the community, and to one another.

Saint Benedict attaches great importance to the place of obedience in the life of the monk, so much so that he calls it "labor obedientiae," that is, "the work of obedience," implying that the practice of monastic obedience is indeed true work for the monk, one of the most indispensable ones in the interval of his monastic life.

In the monastery, the monk or nun hears the call to obedience every day. Indeed, by putting into daily practice the "work of obedience" the monk, in the words of Saint Benedict, "becomes acceptable to God and pleasant to the men around him." Saint Benedict clearly specifies that the obedience shown to the abbot and to one another is shown to God directly—for the gospels remind us, "Whoever listens to you listens to me" (Luke 10:16).

"Monastic obedience," to quote from Dom Adalbert de Vogue (a longtime student of the Rule of Saint Benedict), "derives its incomparable value from this twofold root: it is both obedience to Christ and obedience in the image of Christ. By obeying him we imitate him. We make his will our own and we participate in his submission to the Father. Obedience is at the heart of the redemption."

And while the monk is encouraged to follow Christ by the humble submission of obedience, Saint Benedict also addresses the abbot and those in position of authority and reminds them of their responsibility in caring for Christ's little flock.

If the Lord designs to entrust to their care the welfare of the monk or nun, they must remember that one day they will be called to give full account on how they exercised their charge. They must rebuke in themselves any propensity to authoritarianism, to pride, and to a dominating tendency. By following the example of Christ, who was always kind and merciful, trusting and forgiving, always the "servant exemplar" to all his disciples, the abbot should be able, in the words of Saint Benedict, "to rejoice in the increase of a good flock," as he guides them through the gospel path to the blessedness of eternal life.

CHAPTER 5

ORA ET LABORA—
Prayer and Work
in Monastic Life

The Work of Prayer

I think there is no labor greater than that of prayer to God. For every time a man wants to pray, his enemies, the demons, want to prevent him, for they know that it is only by turning him from prayer that they can hinder his journey. Whatever good work a man undertakes, if he perseveres in it, he will attain rest. But prayer is warfare to the last breath.

ABBA AGATHON, *THE SAYINGS OF THE DESERT FATHERS*

After a long spell of prayer, do not say that nothing has been gained, for you have already achieved something. For, after all, what higher good is there than to cling to the Lord and to persevere in unceasing union with him?

SAINT JOHN CLIMACUS, *THE LADDER OF DIVINE ASCENT*

Prayer is the inner symphony in the life of the monk. It's the one purpose, the aim toward which all his strength and efforts are directed. According to Saint Benedict, a man who enters a monastery does it primarily with the intention of seeking God. Everything else is secondary to this, subordinated to this end. How does the monk seek God; how does he look for him in this life? How is this life expressed? Like all Christians, the monk has first received the gift of faith. He is rooted in it, and it is ultimately faith that evokes and nurtures his total response to God. Faith tells him that God is not just an abstract idea or an ethereal being, but a living God in whose presence he stands.

The fact that God became human is the great mystery of Christianity, for God became human that humankind might become God. This speaks of the unfathomable love and care of God for his creatures. We humans have become partakers of the nature of God, as Saint Peter tells us, by being raised to the dignity of "divine sonship" by adoption. God, in his love, has created the possibility for people to relate to him in a new way. God pours his Holy Spirit into every human being, and it is by this Spirit that we are able to say, "Abba, Father."

In the light of this new relationship to God, one can explain the life of the monk, for he understands this relation of filial sonship to the Father and hears in the depths of his heart the divine invitation to live solely for God and with him. "Come," God says, "I am life." The

Our Father in heaven...

monk's life, then, becomes a natural unfolding of this new, intimate friendship with God. This relationship finds its expression in the life of prayer, which best expresses the totality of this involvement of humans with God. Therefore, it is natural that the whole life of the Christian monk should gravitate toward prayer, toward living in a close and conscious union with God.

To understand this even more clearly, we must look to what the sacred Scriptures say about prayer, for the word of God is the daily bread of the monk. Saint Paul, in his First Letter to the Thessalonians, counsels all Christians to "pray without ceasing." The monk, who is simply an ordinary Christian, takes this counsel to heart and makes of it the very reason for his life. Prayer becomes the very center and source of his being, the perspective from which he looks at all things, the end toward which his whole life tends. Following the invitation of the divine master, "Go to your inner room, close the door, and pray to your Father in secret" (Matthew 6:6), the monk's life is marked by this continual journey into the depths of his heart to seek the face of God. This is perhaps the chief characteristic distinguishing the monastic life from other forms of Christian life: the intensity of the monk's interior journey and the profundity from which he is called to pray.

Prayer opens our hearts to the reality of God and others. For the monk, God and humankind are not two separate concerns but very much one; one being part of the other. Instead of dichotomizing, prayer brings all things into unity, helping one see the underlying interrelation of all things. In the light of God, one comes to see all things as one. Prayer, when perfected by grace, leads one to recognize the presence of Christ in every human being.

Although prayer is the daily occupation of the monk, it is by no means easy for him (or any other Christian, for that matter). It is true that one can experience deep joy and peace in prayer, but it is often a struggle. One does not always find oneself ready to pray. Even in a monastery, there are the daily worries, vicissitudes, and distractions of ordinary living; these can be obstacles to real prayer. One often feels lazy, bored, and almost incapable of going down into one's heart to pray. And perhaps the most difficult of all is the need to face oneself as one is before God. This, more than anything else, discourages people from prayer. It is even more difficult to know that after having acknowledged what one is, one has to do something about it.

Prayer is rooted in the experience of daily life. Monks face the same difficulties that others do in trying to pray. This struggle is daily. However, monastics realize that the "kingdom of heaven suffers violence," that it is natural that one should struggle to possess it. Monks and other Christians have heard Christ saying to his disciples that one must "watch and pray" so as not to fall into the subtle traps of the evil one. Very often (like their predecessors the Desert Fathers) monks have to confront the evil one under many faces. They are then reminded of the truth of Christ's words that there are "certain demons that can be conquered only by fasting and prayer."

All Christian life is a call to conversion, to *metanoia*, to the rebirth and blossoming of the new person in Christ. This, of course, does not happen immediately. It is an ongoing process, something that should be happening every day of our lives. It is here that monks do a service to the church of God and to society at large: We remind others of these fundamental values and of our calling to total conversion in order to partake of the divine life and thus become new beings in Christ. Christianity makes sense only in the light of this possible transformation. In the busyness of everyday living, it is easy to forget the fundamental aims and direction of all Christian living. Monks, by trying to live a very ordinary life of fidelity and prayer, of simplicity and work, of discipline, silence, and hospitality, strive to work out this process of conversion and, moved by the Holy Spirit, orient the totality of our human existence toward God, the one absolute. Monks make an effort to remind themselves daily they must walk the "narrow way" of the gospel, conscious that this leads one to the final transformation in Christ.

We are conscious that all Christians are called to the same end in one way or another. The gospel of Christ is not addressed only to monks or any other particular group, but equally to all people without distinction. In a sense, there is no such thing as a monastic spirituality, but only a Christian spirituality derived directly from the teachings of the gospel. Monks, by taking to heart the counsel of the gospel, by giving ourselves seriously to a life of prayer, seeking only the "one thing necessary," do the service of reminding all our fellow human beings of the essence of the Christian life.

That prayer has great power
Which a person makes with all his might.
It makes a sour heart sweet,
A sad heart merry,
A poor heart rich,
A foolish heart wise,
A timid heart brave,
A sick heart well,
A blind heart full of sight,
A cold heart ardent.
It draws down the great God into the little heart,
It drives the hungry soul up into the fullness of God.
It brings together two lovesrs,
God and the soul,
In a wondrous place where they speak much of love.
    Mechthilde of Magdeburg, thirteenth-century Beguine

The Work of God *(The Opus Dei)*

The true monk should have prayer and
psalmody continually in his heart.
ABBA EPIPHANIUS, *THE SAYINGS OF THE DESERT FATHERS*

The psalms are the true garden of the solitary
and the Scriptures are his paradise.
THOMAS MERTON, *THOUGHTS IN SOLITUDE*

The Psalter (as the first Book of Psalms is commonly called by monks) is a place where God and the monk meet daily. By praying the words of the psalms, the monk shares in the experience of the Chosen People of the Bible, for whom the psalms were their daily prayers. In the psalms the monk hears the supplications of the people of God; their cries of fear, anguish, and suffering; their expressions of joy, praise, and thanksgiving; and even at times the cries of desperation, resentment, and revolt against God. All human feelings and experience are found and expressed somewhere in the psalms.

The Psalms, more than any other book of prayers, express the interaction between God and humanity since the first moments of creation. For the monk, to pray the psalms is to enter into this dialogue through history. This history reveals to us God's actions in the midst and on behalf of his people. God creates man and woman; and he calls them to a life of union with him. When they disobey, God throws them out of paradise, but he promises them a redeemer. In the meantime, God watches over his people and enters into an alliance with them, an alliance that ultimately finds its fulfillment with the arrival of the promised Savior.

All this and more is expressed and prayed in the psalms. This divine reality, revealed and encountered there, becomes the manna from above that daily nourishes the monk's inner life. Through the psalms, the monk expresses to God not only the totality of his own sentiments, but of the whole of humanity. The psalms are a cry to God for liberation on behalf of all people.

Saint Benedict arranged the daily monastic schedule around the Work of God, which he considered the chief occupation of the monk. The Work of God—or the Divine Office, as it was later called—consisted of eight periods of formal prayer distributed throughout the day, of which the psalms were the main component. Besides the psalms, there also were hymns, readings, responses, and other prayers, but psalmody, the singing of the psalms, constituted the main part of the Work of God. Daily psalm singing played a central role for Saint Benedict and the early monks; not so much as a method of prayer, but as a true experience of God in prayer. Psalmody, said Thomas Merton, "brings us in direct contact with him whom we seek." Psalmody, in other words, was the ordinary means for the monk to approach the presence of the living God. Thus, Saint Benedict admonishes the monk that "nothing must be preferred or take precedence to the Work of God."

The ancient monks used to sing the 150 psalms in one day, sometimes several times in one day. Saint Benedict, with his usual sense of balance and moderation, distributed the 150 psalms throughout the span of a week. Saint Benedict also distributed the order of the psalms according to the characters of the different hours of the day and the rhythm of the seasons, especially the liturgical seasons. The first Office of the day was the night Office now called vigils, celebrated in the time of Saint Benedict around 2 a.m. Today some monasteries and individual monks still retain the night character of this Office. Others celebrate it late at night before retiring to bed, and

others in the very early hours of the morning. The Office of lauds follows, in which the psalms and canticles of praise are sung, which is why the Office is sometimes called Morning Praise.

The little hours—the Offices of prime, terce, sext, and none—were recited during the first, third, sixth, and ninth hours of the day. These hours corresponded approximately to our present 6 a.m., 9 a.m., noon, and 3 p.m., depending on the particular season of the year. Today prime has been suppressed in most monasteries because it is simply a duplication of the more important hour of lauds. In some monasteries, following the liturgical adaptations of the Church after the last Ecumenical Council, keep only one little hour, which is usually celebrated at noon and is called the Noonday Office.

The hour of vespers—considered by some to be the most solemn Office of the day—was celebrated at sunset. Vespers, one of the most beautiful Offices of the monastic day, originated in the tradition of Jewish synagogue worship, which was adapted and continued by the early Christians and monks of the primitive Church. Psalm 140 speaks of the "evening sacrifice," and is considered the official psalm of vespers. Besides Psalm 140 and various other psalms, the *Phos Hilaron,* a second-century hymn to Christ, is sung every day in our monastery. This beautiful hymn refers to Christ as the "evening light." The Office concludes with the Magnificat, Mary's song of praise to God for his goodness and wonders. The last Office of the monastic day, compline, is celebrated at day's end just before retiring, while darkness covers the earth. The psalms of compline are the same every day: Psalms 4, 90, and 133. With the proper hymn of the hour, they quite appropriately constitute the night prayer of the monk.

The psalms, as they were in the synagogue and early Church, are always sung, whether in monasteries by the monastic community or in the hermitage by the monk alone. The psalms were composed to be sung in praise of God, and they convey their true meaning only when they are sung. It is not always as important how beautifully they are sung as how prayerfully and fervently.

As the days, months, and years of life pass and are shaped ever more deeply by the worship of God through the daily chanting of the psalms, he comes to realize in his innermost being the truth of the words of the psalmist:

How lovely is your dwelling place,
Lord, God of hosts....
They are indeed blessed,
those who dwell in your house
forever singing your praise.
    Psalm 84:1, 4, sung version

The Divine Office is at the same time the word of God for man and the work of man for God. It is God's revelation of himself in human accents, it is man's debt repaid to him in the medium of sacrifice.
    Dom Hubert Van Zeller, *The Holy Rule*

Vigils *Psalms, Prayers, Hymns, Silent meditation*

I rise before dawn and cry out;
I put my hope in your words.
My eyes greet the night watches
As I meditate on your promise.

PSALM 119:147–148

The night, inside or outside of the monastery, is impregnated with mystery. It is like a deep abyss where we don't see a boundary. Sometimes I think of the silence of night as that of the empty tomb on Easter Sunday; mysterious, yes, but so full of life. I love our long, quiet nights. They are so much part of our daily life that I can't bear it when their silence is invaded, assaulted, or infringed upon. Night's silence is sacred in the monastery. It must be, for it is the time for God alone.

From the early beginnings of monasticism, the first monks and nuns applied themselves to the practice of keeping vigils. They rose before dawn and awaited the arrival of the new day in prayer. This was nothing new to them, for the first Christians, following Jesus' counsel, were fervent in observing what was then called "the watches of the night." Watch and pray, for the Lord shall come as a thief in the night, according to the Bible. Alertness, watchfulness, and vigilance were teachings that came straight from the gospels, admonitions which the early monks and nuns took to heart. *Deus meus ad te de luce vigilo.* ("My God, I keep watch and wait upon you before the arrival of the Light.")

Today, the Office of Vigils is observed in different fashions depending on the custom of the particular monastery or hermit. Some anticipate their vigils the night before, others observe them in the middle of the night, and others pray them just before the arrival of the dawn. No matter how and when the vigils are prayed, they always retain their nightly character. Saint John Chrysostom recalled the night vigils of the early monks: "Just as they rise, they intone the psalms of David, and sing them with such sweet harmony!

There is no harp, or flute, or any other instrument that can render a similar sound to theirs! In the silence and solitude of night, their prayer rises like that of the saints. They sing with the angels, yes, with the angels, the *Laudate Dominum de coelis*, while the rest of us are still in our deep sleep, or semi-asleep, dreaming of worldly cares." (Homily XIV)

The Office of Vigils always starts with "*Domine labia mea aperies*" ("O Lord, open my lips"). The monk faces the altar and repeats it three times as prescribed in the Rule. The others respond: "And my mouth shall proclaim your praise." The invitatory, Psalm 94, follows. Since vigils is the first Office of the day, a great deal of its opening consists of an invitation to worship and adoration. The hymn follows and the psalmody starts. The psalmody at vigils keeps a restrained character, vigilant and appropriate for that hour of day. In many cases the psalms are recited by a monk alone, by the light of a flickering candle, while the others listen and pray. There are long, silent pauses in between psalms and readings. After the psalmody lessons from the Scriptures and the Fathers are read, followed by the responses. On Sundays, a resurrection gospel is proclaimed, followed by the *Te Deum* or *Te Decet Laus*, which brings the Vigil Office to a close. As the Office of

Vigils comes to an end, the first light of day begins to appear on the horizon. A new day begins; a day full of promise, a day to be lived for God, for our brothers and sisters in Christ scattered around all corners of the globe. The monk awaits the light of day in prayer and in joy, for he knows himself to be one of "the children of light.

Awake all you who are asleep,
And rise from among the dead.
For Christ is Risen from the dead
And he shall give us light.

The night is dark for unbelievers, O Christ,
But for the faithful there is light in the truth of your words.
Therefore, we keep vigil for You.
Awaiting your coming, O Lord.
    OFFICE OF VIGILS, OUR LADY OF THE RESURRECTION MONASTERY

Lauds *(A service of morning prayer*
Praise   5 - 6

The beauty of the rising sun
Begins to tint the world with light,
Awakened nature glows with life
As form and color reappear.

Lord Jesus Christ, You far surpass
The sun that shines since time began;
We turn to You with joyous song
That You may bless us with your smile.
    PERGRATA MUNDI, LAUDS HYMN FOR TUESDAY

Saint Benedict points out in the Rule that lauds, the Office of morning praise, must be sung at the moment one perceives the first rays from the sun, *illucescente aurora*. Daybreak, when the freshness of dawn is felt and the dewdrops still find repose on the treetops, is the appointed time to offer the Lord our morning supplication. It is a blessed moment of the day, for the sun, a symbol of the eternal Sun of Justice, is just appearing on the horizon. It recalls another early morning, when Christ, our true Light, rose from the dead. The Office of Lauds, especially on Sundays, is enfolded in the mystery of the resurrection. With the holy myrrh-bearer women, we approach the tomb that held life. We sit by its side, and with joyful voices we proclaim to the world that Christ is indeed risen.

The Office begins with "*Deus in adjutorium meun intende*" ("O Lord, come to my assistance"). The choir replies: "Lord, make haste to help me." The doxology and hymn of the day follows. The hymn can be from the ordinary of the day, depending on the day and week; it can be seasonal, such as Advent, Lent, or paschaltime; or it can be from the proper of a feast or saint. The hymn serves as an introduction to the Office; it conveys its theme and opens our hearts to praise. It is a pity that some monasteries, being a bit legalistic about the Rule, postpone the singing of the hymn until the psalmody is  completed. (Saint Benedict places the hymn after the short reading-response following the psalmody.) After the liturgical adaptations from the Vatican Council, the church reassigned the hymns to the entry of all the Offices, where they properly belong. When the time comes to decide the format or time of a certain Office, he gives a great deal of latitude to the abbot or the person in charge of the responsibility for the *Opus Dei*. He says in chapter 18 of his Rule that if this arrangement is unsatisfactory to anyone, he may do otherwise if he has thought of a better one.

After the hymn of the hour or day, we proceed to psalmodize until the moment of the lesson from the Scriptures. While the psalms are sung in English here, the antiphons are sung in Latin. They are simple and basic to understand, and besides, they provide us with the proper Gregorian mode for singing their correspondent psalm. After the lesson from the Scriptures, a few minutes of silence follow for meditation on the word of God. Again, this can become terribly mechanical in those monasteries where there is no pause for prayer or where the lesson is read in Latin. Not only that, but they use the same old lessons over and over again, never taking advantage of the richness and diversity now provided by the new breviary. This is mostly due to a false belief that true fidelity demands a refusal

to change or adapt to new circumstances. After the meditation on the Scripture lesson, a simple or solemn response follows depending on the feast or occasion. The Gregorian response is always sung in Latin.

Lauds conclude with the *Benedictus Canticle*, which lovingly proclaims: "In the tender compassion of our God the dawn from on high shall break upon us, to shine on those who dwell in darkness and the shadow of death, and to guide our feet into the way of peace." The intercessions and the Our Father follow. Our morning praise closes with the prayer of the day.

The sun is erstwhile on high, shining on the world. People everywhere are awakening to face the pains and joys of a new day. The monk carries in his heart, in his prayer, the needs and sufferings of the entire world. This is his particular call. This is what God asks of him. Gazing at the light from on high, the monk is confident that all is well. For he, the giver of light, who makes the sun shine on the virtuous and the malevolent, is mindful of the individual needs of all his children. As morning begins, and the day proceeds through its course, we pray often: "*Exsurge Christe, adjuva nos* (Rise, O Christ, quickly, and come to our aid)."

Sext Noon – Psalms

O true noon-day
When warmth and light are at their peak
And the sun at its zenith
And no shadows fall;
When stagnant waters dry up
And their fetid odors disperse.
O never-ending solstice
When daylight lasts forever.
O noon-day light,
Marked with the mildness of spring,
Stamped with summer's bold beauty,
Enriched with autumn's fruit,
And (lest I seem to forget)
Calm with winter's rest from toil.
    SAINT BERNARD

$\mathcal{T}$he quiet of noon arrives daily, and is seen seemingly uneventful. A profound silence fills the monastery, the sky, the gardens, and the surrounding fields. The bells peal the Angelus and they beckon us once more to prayer. After several hours of intense work, it is a welcome pause. One thanks God for the gift of the past hours, for what was accomplished in them and for all that is waiting to be done:

Almighty Ruler, God of Truth,
From whom the ordered seasons flow,
The splendor of the morning sun,
The noonday heat which you bestow.
    RECTOR POTENS, *HYMN FOR THE HOUR OF SEXT*

Noonday reminds one of many things, in particular, of the mystery of time. How fleeting the hours are! Life is often a struggle. And noontime accentuates the weariness, the burdens of the day. The monk has humbly cast his lot among the poor and the lowly, among those who occupy the last place in society. We have nothing to count on except God's mercy. We only find rest, shelter, refuge, and comfort under the shadow of his wings. I delight in having this noonday pause for prayer. Though short, it lifts up my spirit, soothes it as I roam through past memories and events. I find peace and tranquility in prayer. This is perhaps why I wish prayer on everyone. Prayer grants us the good fortune to bathe our tired spirit in God's presence, in the luminous rays of his light, in the warm heat of his love. These are my thoughts, rambling and free, as I steep myself into the quiet of the hour.

Vespers

Let my prayer be incense before you;
my uplifted hands an evening offering.
    PSALM 141:2

The sun begins its daily descent, the end of the day is near. The peace of the evening seems to envelop the monastic enclosure. In the early days, the Christians of the Church of Jerusalem used to rush to the church of the Holy Sepulchre and spend the remaining evening hours in prayer. It was the hora incensi, the hour to offer the evening incense, as Saint Ambrose describes it. It was also the time of the lucernarium, when the first evening lamps were lit. The Office of Vespers is an ancient rite of prayer, rooted in the prayer of

the synagogue itself, where it has its origins. After the resurrection of Jesus, the apostles and the first disciples continued to pray in the evening, following the Jewish custom. Soon that prayer took on a different character altogether. There were no longer offerings of animal sacrifices, as in the past. Instead, the sacrifice of Christ on the cross was commemorated. Recalling the exhortation from the Letter to the Hebrews, this was the evening sacrifice they offered to God:

"Now Christ has come, as the high priest of all the blessings that were to come....He has entered the sanctuary once and for all, taking with him not the blood of goats and bull calves, but his own blood, having won an eternal redemption for us....The blood of Christ, who offered himself as the perfect sacrifice to God through the eternal Spirit, can purify our inner self from our daily shortcomings so that we can offer a sacrifice of praise to the living God."

The hour of vespers is observed in the monastery at the most solemn hour of the day. There is something quietly majestic about it. At sunset, when the rays from the sun begin to withdraw from our sight, the bells of the monastery summon us to our evening praise. The many candles and the oil lamps in front of our icons are lit. The sweet scent of incense pervades the air. Chanting begins slowly with the Byzantine invocation: "Blessed is our God, now and always, and unto ages of ages." We all respond with a solemn "Amen." The opening hymn and the psalmody follows, just as we did at morning lauds, with the antiphons in Latin and the psalms in English. Psalm 140, which speaks of the "evening sacrifice," is sung every day in the Byzantine tradition. It is the vespers Psalm *par excellence*. After Psalm 140, a special prayer of the light is offered, followed by the *Phos Hilaron*, one of the oldest hymns to Christ and one of the most beautiful of all the Christian hymnology. The hymn praises Christ as our "evening light" who comes to lighten our darkness:

Now that we come to the setting of the sun,
beholding the evening light,
we sing our hymn to God:
The Father, Son, and Holy Spirit.

An appropriate lesson from the Scriptures is read and then the electric lights are put out for a few minutes of silent meditation. It is a solemn moment of the day. In the evening darkness, we are alone with God, surrounded by the *Theotokos* and the saints as our only company. There is only a response on solemn festival days. On ordinary days, we offer the depth of our silence as our sole response. The lights are lit again, and the Magnificat is intoned. We sing the Magnificat accompanied by the Byzantine antiphon: "More honorable than the cherubim, and more glorious beyond compare than the seraphim. Remaining a virgin you gave birth to God the Word, true *Theotokos* we magnify you." This antiphon is sung here daily, following the Byzantine usage. On feast days and solemnities, the Latin Gregorian antiphon or the proper Troparion replaces this otherwise daily antiphon. During the Magnificat on feast days, all the icons in the chapel are incensed, as they are during Psalm 140.

Our eventide Office comes to its conclusion in the same manner as morning lauds, with final intercessions, the Our Father and the final prayer. A final blessing and a hymn to our Lady closes the evening Office, followed by the veneration of our icons, something that is part of the daily ritual of this monastery.

The last rays from the sun have vanished, and dusk starts to descend upon us. The early shadows quietly delineate the silhouettes of our trees, our buildings, and the cross high on the bell tower. There is no room for fear. Christ, our light, is among us, to protect us from the gloom of our own darkness, from the advances of the evil one. The Lord is palpably there, close by, to guide our feet into the ways of peace.

Compline

God, who made the earth and heaven,
Darkness and light:
You the day for work have given,
For rest the night.
May your angel guards defend us,
Slumber sweet your mercy send us,
Holy dreams and hopes attend us
All through the night.

REGINALD HEBER

It is an exquisite summer night. A poet certainly would feel inspired by the magic of the moment, seized by the fragrance emanating from our gardens and the surrounding fields. As I look at the wide-open sky, every star seems to have taken its rightful place in the heavens. A bright moon accompanies them, bathing the darkness with its own startling clarity. Throughout the ages, *au clair de la lune* has inspired composers, poets, writers, even monks!

There is something calming about the nighttime that inspires silence, recollection, and peaceful reflection. The night, though obscure and mysterious, displays a transparency in its darkness. That is its very mystery.

The evening meal has finished and the dishes have been piled up in the sink. The day's journey comes to its conclusion.

The monastery bells ring for the last Office of the day, summoning us to compline. After that, the bells and everyone within the monastic enclosure shall remain utterly silent until the following day. In the chapel, the only lights are those in front of the main icons of the Savior and the *Theotokos*. Compline is a short, self-effacing Office. There is no pomp in its ritual, only a sense of spareness and simplicity, a feeling of close intimacy. To enhance the simplicity of this Completorium Office, Saint Benedict deliberately makes it repetitive in its format and content. There is no variation in the psalms. The three assigned psalms—numbers 4, 90, and 133—are repeated every night. The only small variation occurs occasionally in the choice of the hymn.

In the quiet of the church, compline begins with a brief examination of conscience. We look back at the events of the day: its joys and sorrows, our conduct and failings, our shortcomings in regard to love and charity. We acknowledge our sinfulness through the Confiteor and humbly beg for pardon to the Father of all mercies. The hymn follows. It is lyrical poetry at its best, a prayer and supplication against the forces of evil and darkness:

O Christ, You are our Light and Day:
Repel the shadows of the night;
You are the true Light, we believe;
You shed your radiance on the blest.

So, we beseech you, holy Lord,
To keep us safe throughout the dark;
In you we may find quiet repose;
Please give to us a tranquil night.

After the hymn, the three above-mentioned psalms are sung and repeated night after night. Since eventually one learns them all by heart, compline is sung in the dark shadows of the night. After the psalmody, the *Capitulum*, or short reading, from the Scriptures follows. There is a pause for silence after which the short response is sung: *In manus tuas Domine, commendo spiritum meam* ("Into your hands, O Lord, I commend my spirit"). How often throughout the years I have made recourse to this short prayer, over and over again! And, I may add, how consoling it has always been! When the end comes, one hopes it shall be the last prayer our souls utter as they move on to other realms. There is a great deal of solace in Jesus' own last words before he departed to the Father.

Compline reaches its peak with elder Simeon's canticle, the *Nunc Dimitis* and its accompanying antiphon: "Save us, O Lord, as we stay awake, and guard us as we sleep. That awake we may keep watch with Christ and asleep rest in his peace." After the canticle, a short prayer follows and the final blessing brings compline to its conclusion. At the end of compline, we tend to the icon of the *Theotokos* and sing one of her seasonal antiphons, usually the *Salve Regina*. With much love and devotion, the monk commends his life, his concerns, and all the intentions entrusted to him, to the care of the Mother of God. She is the *Mater Misericordiae* who watches day and night over all his children. She is also *Vita, Dulcedo et Spes nostra*: the source of life and all sweetness, and the reason for our hope. We can take leave for the night and still feel secure, for we place our trust in her unfailing protection. The *Theotokos* stands between heaven and earth. She is the ladder by which each of us can ascend to God.

After our Lady's antiphon, as we bow to the altar and leave the chapel, we are sprinkled with holy water. Silently, we depart for the repose of the night. The day's journey has ended by our singing God's praises and commending ourselves to the intercession of the holy Mother of God. As we enter into the secrecy of the night silence, we seek quiet repose for our tired bodies and spiritual refreshment for our souls. We proceed to our rest, yet we remain vigilant, for tonight, as on every other night, the monk must always heed to the Lord's admonition: Watch and pray. Be ready, for the Lord shall come as a thief in the night.

The Work and Sound of Praise: The Chant

When you sing with your voice, a moment comes when you stop singing; then it is the moment to begin singing with your life, and you will never stop singing.

SAINT AUGUSTINE

Beautiful sound reinforces the power of beautiful words.

G. VAN DER LEEUW, *SACRED AND PROFANE BEAUTY*

The worship of God, the principal occupation of the monk, is accomplished daily in the celebration of the Divine Office and the Eucharist. This worship of God, in the thought of Saint Benedict, should be accomplished by the monk with the reverence, respect, profound humility, and beauty that is owed to God. Saint Benedict cites Psalm 138, "In the presence of angels to you I sing," then he says to the monk, "Let us consider, then, how we ought to behave in the presence of God and his angels, and let us stand to sing the psalms in such a way that our minds are in harmony with our voices."

The monastic chant, in particular the Gregorian chant, which is perhaps the best expression of the monastic chant in the West, plays an important role in enhancing the monk's worship of God. In the words of an expert, Dom Gajard, the famous choirmaster of

the Abbey of Solesmes: "the chant is both prayer and liturgy; it is the liturgical prayer celebrated in song." The function of the chant in the liturgy is to be a vehicle of prayer, a vehicle that raises the monk's soul to express the praise of God in the most beautiful way possible.

The Gregorian chant, because of its simplicity and beauty, has served well throughout the centuries as monks' normal tool of enhancing the worship of God in the liturgy. First of all, it is important to notice that there is an intrinsic unity between the notes of the chant and the text of the liturgy. Sounds and words are intimately connected in Gregorian chant; one cannot exist without the other. The words give meaning to the music and convert the chant into a song that prays. As Dom Gajard used to say, "Gregorian chant above all things is prayer, and nothing but prayer. It is sung and directed to God alone."

The Gregorian repertoire is so ancient and vast that it provides the diversity of expression required by the various liturgical seasons and feast days of the Church year. For instance, the Gregorian repertoire of Advent and Christmas is very different from that of Lent and Easter, and these two are also different from that which is now called Ordinary Time. The chant grew up in the Latin Church throughout the centuries, and it was particularly cultivated in monasteries as the most fitting form of worship and praise. There are various traditions of chants, depending on their places of origin: the Roman chant, the Mozarabic chant from Spain, the Ambrosian chant from Milan, the Sarum chant from England, and of course the Gregorian chant, the best-known of all of them, which has survived up to our own time.

The melodies of the Gregorian chants are written according to modes, not in the traditional tonal music known to us today. Consequently, the chants contain a colorful, expressive character all their own. There are eight modes in the Gregorian chant, each with a particular flavor, which provide for this wonderful variety of expression, color, and character. The Gregorian chant is also different from other music in that it has no tempo, only rhythm. In many ways, the subtly modal character of the free-rhythm chant makes the Gregorian chant perfectly apt as the sung expression of prayer. It is a form of music whose very structure is geared to prayer and leads to contemplation. In comparison to other church music, the purity of Gregorian melody is such that besides articulating the richness of the liturgical text, it creates a serene climate that allows the monk's soul to be raised tranquilly and naturally up to the heights of contemplation, deep into the mystery of God.

That which happens in Liturgy is impossible without music, without poetry, without gesture, without emotion. There a man is brought to that which is true. He should be gratified in his arms, legs, eyes, ears, head, and heart: he should rise, genuflect, sing, listen, close his eyes, join hands, be silent....Pity the man who must do all this without music because he has unlearned how to sing...without gesture because he has forgotten he has a body...without a festive air because he no longer likes to adorn.

BERNARD HUYBERS, *THE PERFORMING AUDIENCE*

The Work of Sacred Reading: *Lectio Divina*

So, as Christians, having learnt from the holy Scriptures and from holy revelations, we know the great goodness of God for those who sincerely take refuge in him and who correct their past faults by repentance, and let us not despair of our salvation.

ABBA PAUL THE SIMPLE, *THE SAYINGS OF THE DESERT FATHERS*

The high esteem in which the words of Scripture were held by the monks as well as the frequent recommendations to memorize and recite the sacred text suggests the presence within desert monasticism of a culture nourished in significant ways on the Scriptures. Besides its place in the public synaxis, Scripture also played a key part in the life of the cells, where it was recited, ruminated, and meditated upon both in small groups of monks and by individuals in solitude.

D. BURTON-CHRISTIE, *THE WORD IN THE DESERT*

To the monk who comes to the monastery with the exclusive purpose of seeking God, Saint Benedict offers different activities that will encourage him in his search. One thoroughly monastic activity, deeply rooted in the tradition, is what is commonly called in the monasteries *lectio divina*, the reflective, prayerful pondering on the word of God in the sacred Scriptures. The monk, moved by the Holy Spirit and encouraged by the Rule, takes time out daily to immerse himself, through prayerful reading, in this living contact with the word of God. During this blessed quiet time of sacred reading, the Holy Spirit takes over. Little by little, in an almost imperceptible way, the Spirit develops in the monk an increasing taste for the word of God and for all things concerning a life of union with God.

The sacred Scriptures then become not just one book among many but, indeed, a very special book. For the monk, as for all Christians, it is not only the book that contains the revealed word of God, it is the book that *is* the word of God. To the monk who, in the silence of his heart, learns to listen to this word with both humility and wonder, the word feeds him mysteriously with the knowledge of God. It encourages him, comforts him, and en-

lightens him as he tries to make progress in his monastic life. The word of God as found in the Scriptures is indeed the daily bread of the monk, for it reveals the depths of God's ineffable mystery, a mystery hidden from all eternity.

Ordinarily, every monastery designates a portion of the day to the practice of *lectio divina*. In many monasteries, this activity usually takes place in the early morning after the Offices. Later on in the afternoon or evening, especially at the end of the day, the monk tries to find time to return again to sacred reading, to quiet repose in the presence of him whom his heart loves and longs for.

The place where the monk usually engages in *lectio divina* is his monastic cell, where he dwells alone with God. Consequently, because of the divine interaction that takes place there, little by little the cell of the monk becomes transformed into a living furnace, where the fire of the Holy Spirit shines brightly day and night.

Although the primary objectives of *lectio divina* is the reading, meditating, and praying over the sacred Scriptures, reading other spiritual texts such as those of the Fathers of the Church, the early Fathers and Mothers of monasticism, the texts of the liturgy, and books on prayer, are also permitted during the time assigned to *lectio*. After all, these books are directly inspired by the Scriptures, and, ultimately, by the Holy Spirit, who cannot be limited to the Scriptures alone for the Spirit indeed breathes where he wills. During the time spent and allotted to *lectio*, the monk's main concern should be using this time wisely to encounter the living God who wishes to speak and reveal himself to the monk's heart. The time of *lectio divina* is time for God alone, and anything else that may interfere with, interrupt, or distract the monk from this one purpose is simply completely out of place. With deep humility, the monk ought to pray to the Holy Spirit daily to guide him in wisely organizing his time of *lectio divina*, so that this truly becomes a time of spiritual rest, of intense, intimate prayer, and of authentic contemplative peace, that allows the monk to leisurely bask in God's presence.

When the monk reads, let him seek for savor and not for science. The Holy Scripture is the well of Jacob from which the waters are drawn which will be poured out later in prayer. Thus there will be no need to go to the oratory to begin to pray; but in reading itself, means will be found for prayer and contemplation.

ABBOT ARNOUL OF BOHERISS, *SPECULUM MONACHORUM*

The Work of Love

Beloved,
let us love one another,
because love is of God;
everyone who loves is begotten by God and knows God.
Whoever is without love does not know God,
for God is love.

    1 JOHN 4:7–8

Love's birthplace is God. There it is born, there it is nourished, there it is reared. There it is at home, not a tourist, but a native. For by God alone is love given, and in him it endures.

    WILLIAM OF SAINT THIERRY, *THE NATURE AND DIGNITY OF LOVE*

An early monk once said the purpose of monastic life was "to cling to that most excellent way, which is love." To truly follow in the footsteps of Christ, the monk has to learn to walk the way of love. And the way of love of the gospels is not easy. It is full of pitfalls. Love is not obtained by simply wanting it, nor is it something we gain merely by willing it. Love is something we work at every day.

The dynamic work of love is the center of monastic life. The heart of the monk, touched by grace, is able to see the painful reality of his brokenness and sinfulness and at the same time encounter the tenderness and loving mercy of a God who alone can forgive him and free him from his own pitfalls.

The deep realization of this personal, all-powerful love of God for the least of his creatures is the dynamic that starts the monk on his monastic journey and that pushes him forward toward its fulfillment. Enveloped as he is by God's love, the monk discovers that to imitate God and follow his ways implies choosing to do the work of love. To become loving and compassionate to all his brothers and sisters and to all created things, as Jesus was, is then his only goal.

This goal, however, is not easily attainable, for the monk, in his poverty, is continually confronted by his limitations. Daily he must begin again and again the work of love. In trying to do the work of love, the monk must not put his trust in his own strength or his own resources. In the midst of the struggle, he must call upon the Holy Spirit, the Spirit of love, to take over and lead the work to completion. He must rely on God alone.

Christ showed us the way of love, and he practiced it to the end by his self-emptying on the cross. The monk, in imitation of his master, is called to put love into practice by means of self-renunciation and by embracing the cross of Christ. According to the monastic tradition, the monk does this concretely by the living out of his monastic profession. By accepting obedience, the monk renounces his own personal will and chooses instead to do only the will of God. By accepting conversion of life, which encompasses the poverty and chastity that are part and parcel of all monastic life, the monk lays aside his claims to ownership and possessions and renounces the blessing of sexual union and fruitfulness. By accepting stability in the monastery, the monk renounces mobility and his independence. Thus, the vows of the monastic life, by which the monk slowly learns to renounce himself and to cleave to God alone, becomes the most pure expression of his love for the Lord.

The work of love is extended and expressed in the daily practice of charity toward the brethren. For the Christian, the love of God and the love of neighbor cannot be separated. People dwelling either inside or outside the monastery are real to the monk, for God has stamped in each person his image and likeness. The monk understands this, so he tries not to exclude anyone, neither the stranger nor even his enemies, from the task of loving them. The work of love is absolutely real, the true meaning of the monk's existence; it absorbs him wholly.

In chapter 53 of the Rule, Saint Benedict mentions quite matter-of-factly that "all guests who arrive at the monastery should be received as Christ, because he will say, 'I was a stranger, and you took me in.' ...When a guest is announced, let him be met by the Superior and the brethren with every mark of charity...let Christ be adored in them as He is also received." Saint Benedict goes on to say, "Let the greatest care be taken, especially in the reception of the poor and travelers, because Christ is received more specially in them." The work of monastic hospitality is very much a part of the work of love, which is the monk's life's task. Hospitality provides a concrete way for the monk to exercise the work of love with persons who live outside the monastery. This is at times a real challenge, but so that there may not remain the slightest doubt about this in the monk's mind, Saint Benedict has assured him that he is showing charity to Christ himself.

Love is not in the first place a sentiment, but a definite work which gets more and more exciting the further one goes; and then from there any "activities" take on their true proportions, they are not so important. The work of love is to see the center [God] in others as their one reality, and then of loving the person in his reality.

Mother Maria, *Her Life in Letters*

The Work of Hospitality

Let all guests who arrive be received as Christ, because He will say: "I was a stranger and you took Me in." And let due honor be shown to all, especially to those "of the household of the faith" (Galatians 6:10) and to wayfarers.

RULE OF SAINT BENEDICT, CHAPTER 53

Through the ancient practice of hospitality, monks share their life with their fellow men. According to the monastic tradition, the doors of a monastery are open to all who come seeking the peace of God, without distinction of belief or background. For the guests the prayer, the silence, and the warm, fraternal welcome make the monastery a real oasis of peace.

Monastic hospitality is different from other forms of hospitality, because it is primarily inspired by faith, not by protocol or any other worldly motive. It is marked by the warmth of Christian love and the simplicity of the Gospel. Saint Benedict counsels the monk to receive guests, who represent Christ, with "with the head bowed down or the whole body prostrate on the ground, let Christ be adored in them as He is also received" (*Rule*, chapter 53).

Monasteries humbly open the doors of their guesthouses to persons of good will who come seeking the peace of God, the *Pax* which remains the ideal of every Benedictine monastery. Guests come alone or in small groups, and they are asked by the monks to respect the contemplative atmosphere of the monastery and its daily schedule. Since prayer and work are the principal activities of all monasteries, the guests are invited to participate in them and to bring their own contributions to the tasks.

Located away from the crowds of the cities and distant enough from noisy roads, a monastery offers its guests:

a place of rest and quiet
a space of silence
an atmosphere of warmth and simplicity
a house of prayer
   where the guests can participate
   in the rhythms of the monastic life
and find time to listen to the word of God
   in the solitude of their hearts.
A brother came to a certain solitary, and when he was going away from him, he said, "Forgive me, Father, for I have made you break your rule." The solitary in turn replied, "My rule is to receive you with hospitality and to send you away in peace."

   H. WADDELL, *THE DESERT FATHERS*

The Work of Our Hands

We urge you, brothers, to progress even more, and to aspire to live a tranquil life, to mind your own affairs, and to work with your [own] hands, as we instructed you, that you may conduct yourselves properly toward outsiders and not depend on anyone.

   1 THESSALONIANS 4:10–12

For then are they monks in truth, if they live by the work of their hands, as did also our forefathers and the Apostles.

   THE RULE OF SAINT BENEDICT, CHAPTER 48

The early monks and nuns supported themselves by the work of their hands, usually weaving mats, hats, rugs, and baskets, which they later sold in the local markets nearby. Following the example and teachings of the apostles, the early monks and nuns seriously applied themselves to the humble task of earning their living, not wishing to be burdens to anyone. Saint Benedict, deeply rooted as he was in the early monastic tradition, handed down the same teaching to his monks. He observes in the Rule that at certain hours of the day, the monk must be engaged in work, manual or otherwise, according to the needs of the monastery, and thus contributes to its support.

Work is an integral part of all human life, be it inside or outside a monastery. What perhaps differentiates the monk's approach to work from that of his fellow humans is the attitude he brings to it. Monastery work is functional. It is not motivated by a desire for a career or for success, or even less by greed. The function of monastic work consists in the imitation of Jesus, the humble carpenter of Nazareth, who came to give us the example of how to live and order our lives. The second function of monastic work is to provide for the needs of the monastery and to help support the monastic community. The third function of monastic work—and this is overlooked by some—is the element of balance that work brings to the daily rhythm of the monastic life. The monk's day-to-day routine consists of trying to strike a balance with prayer and work, reading, study, and rest. This balance is essential, for it contributes to freeing the monk's mind and heart for the purpose for which he came to the monastery, that is, communion with God. Monastic work, though done in the solitude and enclosure of a monastery, adds another positive, redemptive dimension to the life of the monk. Through it the monk is permitted to share in the suffering, hardness, and insecurities of workers all around the world. It allows him to express his solidarity with all those who also must earn their daily bread with the sweat of their brows.

The concrete aspects of monastery work are many. The work depends on the practical needs of the place and the community, the commands of obedience, and the particular talents of the individual monk. First of all, there is the general maintenance of the monastic buildings and property. Then there is the cleaning and other regular work of the various departments of a monastery: the chapel, sacristy, library, refectory, kitchen, laundry, and guesthouse. There is also the heavy manual labor required on the farm, in the gardens, for wood splitting and with other outdoor chores. The particular industry of each monastery, the product of the monks' hands—foods, icons, and more—is marketed to support the monastery. Then there are Offices and tasks assigned to individual monks, such as porter, guest master, cellarer, archivist, librarian, cook, carpenter, electrician, infirmarian, and other roles similar to those of any ordinary household.

The work of our small farm and gardens is an ever-engaging task. Farming may not always be very remunerative, but I have found that it is one of the instruments that keeps us monks grounded in reality, making us grow daily in the awareness of our total dependence on God. For this reason, monks usually choose to live close to the soil—and thus to the God who makes it fertile. Here at Our Lady of the Resurrection, we now raise only sheep and a few chickens, which provide us with eggs for the table year-round. Cultivating our gardens is equally demanding work, but a bit more remunerative, since it provides foods for the table and products to sell weekly at the local farmer's market in Millbrook and in Arlington, New York.

Like other local farmers, our monastery has a small stand at the market where we sell the products from our farm and gardens: eggs, dips, herbal vinegars, jams and marmalades, honey, chutneys and sauces, relishes and pickles, dried culinary herbs, and a variety of prepared food. This weekly market experience is a rather humble and sober one, and follows the tradition of the early desert monks and nuns. And this experience provides me also a better understanding of chapter 5 of the Rule, where Saint Benedict counsels monks to avoid greed in pricing and to sell their wares a little bit lower than people outside the monastery, so that in all things God may be glorified. This is not always simple or easy; it demands a certain amount of discretion and discernment, virtues greatly encouraged by the Rule.

But besides reinforcing virtues encouraged by the Rule, the weekly market experience is deeply satisfying in that it allows a monk to share the same tensions, frustrations, hard work, joys, and rewards of the other local farmers. This creates a certain solidarity among all of us. When I first began offering our monastery wares, there were many who blinked in disbelief. They didn't know what to make of a monk's presence in their midst. Today, however, the other sales people have bonded in friendship with me, understanding better that we monks share the same uncertainty and struggles in trying to earn an income with the work of our hands. The level of acceptance is such that at times some of them approach me to exchange some of their produce with me according to our mutual needs or confide a problem and then ask me to pray for them.

Work is an inescapable feature of daily monastic living. A good monk does not seek to avoid it; instead, he approaches it with a humility that fosters a prayerful attitude to permeate his work. He lets the joys and sufferings experienced during work time find places in his daily prayers, so that, as Saint Benedict counsels in the Rule, "God may be glorified in all things."

Go to a monastery expecting to see other worldly men and women, and you will be disappointed and possibly scandalized by the time spent there in such mundane tasks as milking cows, manuring fields, pitching hay, baking bread, keeping bees, making jelly. Yet the secret of holiness, wholeness, and health is there, for the life is a carefully, even artistically, constructed dialogue of the spirit with creation. Out of that dialogue grows true humanness.

James Deschene, *The Mystic and the Monk: Holiness and Wholeness*

PART II

THE SEASONAL

RHYTHMS OF

Monastic

LIFE

CHAPTER 6
Winter Liturgical Cycle

Advent

Long is our winter;
Dark is our night;
Come, set us free,
O Saving Light!
    Fifteenth-century German hymn

*A*s we enter into the season of Advent, our winter days grow shorter, the air grows colder, and a quiet stillness settles on the physical world at large. All living things that must survive the winter out-of-doors draw deep into themselves. The trees retract their sap, the forest animals hibernate, and the living creatures that continue to move around in the cold, snow-covered world take care to conceal their food stores.

Just as nature retreats deep into itself during the winter months, so the Christian is invited to turn inward during the blessed time

of Advent in preparation for the Lord's coming. This inner preparation—helped by prayer, silence, Bible readings, and good works—is essential if we are to celebrate in a worthy manner the solemn commemoration of the Lord's birth on Christmas Day and during the whole of the Christmas season.

Advent is a quiet, contemplative time of waiting for the light that will come and shine on us on Christmas Day, rescuing us from the great darkness and hopelessness we experience in our daily lives. Advent, then, is a very special season of hope that links the coming of the promised Messiah in Jesus with the coming of Christ into our own hearts after a period of preparation, and with the coming of Christ again at the end of time. Like other seasons of the liturgical year, Advent commemorates something of the past in order to heighten our awareness of the same mystery at work in our own present lives and to fill us with hope about the still-awaited future.

The Eastern Christian tradition sees the Advent season as a time of waiting for the light that will first shine forth at Christmas and reach its peak on Epiphany, the feast of Lights. The beautiful Isaiah text is then proclaimed during liturgy: "Arise! Shine, for your light has come, the glory of the LORD has dawned upon you....Upon you the LORD will dawn, and over you his glory will be seen" (Isaiah 60:1–2).

It is a lovely thing to see that in the Northern Hemisphere, Christ's birth coincides with the victory of light over darkness in the physical world. After the winter solstice, about December 22, daylight slowly begins to lengthen, filling us with a sense of expectancy and promise. Likewise, during our Advent journey, our longing intensifies for the true Light who will be revealed on Christmas Day, thenceforth dispelling the darkness from the innermost parts of our hearts. During the long Advent nights, the

Church of the East prays in one of its liturgical texts, "To those who are caught in the night straying into the works of darkness, grant, O Christ, your light and your blessings." Because we feel ourselves caught in an abyss of fear and darkness, we become deeply aware of our basic instinctual need for light, for the light of truth that is Christ (John 14:6). As we arrive at the end of our Advent journey and enter into the mystery of Christ's birth, "we rejoice with great joy" for, as another Byzantine text proclaims, "Our Savior, the Day-springs from on high, has visited us, and we who were in darkness and shadows have found the truth." On Christmas Day, the intense longing of our Advent prayer "Come, Lord Jesus" is fulfilled, our hope becomes a promise renewed, and our darkness is vanquished by the radiant splendor of God's light.

Lord Jesus Christ,
Son of God and son of Mary,
You are the radiant start of morning.
Come and deliver us from our fears
And the darkness in our everyday lives.
As the Church in earlier times
Once cried for you, we cry again with one voice:
Come, Lord Jesus, come!
Look with mercy upon us
Who await your coming,
And make shine on us
Your saving light.

The Advent Journey

Eternal God who made the stars,
Your people's everlasting light!
O Lord, Redeemer, save us all,
And hear your servants when they call.

You came with healing power to save
A world that languished, self-condemned:
The wounds of sin were wide and deep,
The cure for guilt was your free gift.

The evening time of life was near
For all the world, when you came forth,
A bridegroom from your nuptial bed
Within the Virgin's spotless womb.

      CONDITOR ALME SIDERUM, ADVENT HYMN FOR VESPERS

As one travels into the rural landscape of New York's Dutchess County during the early days of winter, one may glimpse the plain from a distance at the unostentatious monastery of Our Lady of the Resurrection. Perched on a hilltop and surrounded by silent wintry woods, our small, secluded monastery lies only a few miles from Millbrook, the nearest village. The brilliant incomparable foliage of autumn has disappeared, and the trees stand stark and bare. One of the delights of early winter is to gaze upon the sunset through the elaborate patterns of branches that partition the pink sky like the elegant tracery of a stained-glass window. The trees, with their bare branches reaching quietly toward the light, seem to share in the pleading of our Advent prayer: "Come, Lord Jesus, come."

Early Christians traditionally prayed with their arms outstretched toward heaven, from where the Lord was to come again.

The winter trees with their branches outstretched is a symbolic reminder to me that the monk, too—especially during this Advent journey—must look at all times toward God in unceasing prayer and reach his open arms toward him with deep desire.

Here in upstate New York, the weather is habitually sharp in early December, sometimes even fiercely cold. Snow may not yet cover the ground, but there is no doubt among us that it is winter. The arrival of the cold in our midst coincides with the arrival of Advent in the monastery.

For us monks, who see ourselves on a pilgrimage throughout life, the Advent season intensifies and deepens the sense of journey. The monastic journey moves forward with expectation toward an arrival, an encounter. The monk, secluded in his monastic solitude, longs and prays expectantly for the blessed coming of the Savior, the Lord Jesus Christ.

In the monastery, there is something special about Advent, and something of it is felt immediately the moment the vespers hymn *Conditor Alme Siderum* is intoned by the choir. Through lilting Gregorian melody, one senses the deep inner joy that comes with the season. From the years of singing time and again the same melodies that the monastic chant provides for each particular feast or season, they have grown into us, giving the awareness of how beautifully they express the rich meaning of the season. The Gregorian chant, sanctified by centuries of monastic use, has its own unique way of conveying something of the mystery commemorated in our liturgical prayer. We must never forget the fact that the chant is not music or melody alone, but it is words *and* music, and the music was written to fit the words, not the other way around, thus making the chant truly a vehicle of prayer. The Gregorian Advent melodies, with their simplicity and serene beauty, have a way of transforming our vocal sounds into acts of praise and adoration to our eternal God, for all his wonderful deeds among us.

Among the antiphons of vespers for the first week of Advent, there is one in particular that nurtures the Advent message of hope and reflects the loveliness of the season: "*In illa die stillabunt montes dulcedinem...* (On that day [of the Lord's coming] sweet wine will flow from the mountains, milk and honey from the hills, alleluia)."

Advent is primarily about the coming of God, and only in a secondary way about our asking, seeking, waiting, and longing. There is hope, because we are unconditionally loved, whatever may be our failures, our tepidity, or our secret despair. The word "come" is a bearer of mystery.

MARIA BOULDING, *THE COMING OF GOD*

The Advent Wreath

Holly and Ivy, Box and Bay
Put in the church on Christmas Day.
FIFTEENTH-CENTURY ENGLISH CAROL

Our small monastery chapel is quite austere (as it should be!), especially during Advent and Lent, when there are no flowers or decorations in it. The only exception is the Advent wreath. In fact, we usually have two Advent wreaths each year, one in the chapel and one at the table in the refectory. These are the only green decorations throughout the monastery before Christmas Day itself.

The custom of the Advent wreath—with its four candles, three purple and one pink—originated in antiquity in the Germanic countries and was passed on from paganism to Christianity. Burning lights and fires during the darkest month (December, or Yule as it was called then) was a part of the folk celebrations enthusiastically anticipated by northern Europeans each year. In the early sixteenth century, during the days of the Reformation, some Christians conceived the idea of introducing this ancient custom, with its symbolism of lights, into their Advent practices, changing it from a pagan custom into a Christian one, Christ being, of course, both the symbol of light and the Light of the World. In Germany the custom took hold among both Protestants and Catholics, was introduced to monasteries of the surrounding region, and then spread from there to the rest of the world.

Here in the monastery, we eagerly await both the preparation of the wreath, usually made of fresh evergreen boughs found on the property, and then the lighting of the first candle on the first Sunday of Advent. In following evenings, before sitting down to supper, we light the candle of that particular week, sing an Advent hymn, and recite the appropriate prayer.

The lighting of the candle provides a moment of intense joy and anticipation, for the candle's peaceful light announces the approaching celebration of the Lord's birth. After the prayer, as we sit to eat, all other lights are put out, and the radiant light from the Advent wreath, with its cheerful and gentle glow, comforts us in an intimate way. It is indeed a very rich moment in the monastic day, a moment filled with promise, peace, prayer, longing, and joyful expectation, for the birth of the Savior is at hand. The cry of the early Church resounds again and again in the heart of the monk: Come, come, Lord Jesus.

In darkness there is no choice.
It is light that enables us to see
the differences between things:
and it is Christ who gives us light.
    C.T. Whitmell

The Annunciation

The angel Gabriel said to Mary in greeting: "Hail, full of grace, the Lord is with you; blessed are you among women."

<small>ADVENT ANTIPHON, THIRD WEEK</small>

During our Advent journey, we often hear the recitation of the annunciation story in the liturgy. The Church, through the liturgy, never ceases to remind us that Advent and Christmas are all about the mystery of the Incarnation. That mystery begins at the moment when Mary, after being greeted by Gabriel and left dumbfounded by his message, utters her fiat in complete assent and submission to the plan of God.

Mary, of course, knew the words of the prophet Isaiah: "the young woman, pregnant and about to bear a son, shall name him Emmanuel." She probably heard this often enough in the synagogue so as to know it by heart. What she never knew, until then, is that Isaiah was speaking of her, that she was eternally destined to bear

Emmanuel, the Father's only Son. As one of the lovely antiphons of the third week of Advent tells us, "This is the good news the prophets foretold: the Savior will be born of the Virgin Mary."

Throughout the whole of Advent, the icon of the annunciation is next to the *Lectionary* in our chapel. Several times a day, as we enter or leave the Oratory, we offer it a profound homage and kiss it reverently. During the liturgy and the Offices, candles are lit next to the icon and incense is offered. As we gaze upon the icon, we see Mary in deep prayer. Suddenly, she is visited by Gabriel, and in her profound humility she seems bewildered by his greeting. Mary is probably frightened by this strange visitor, as it is not every day that one is greeted by an angel.

If Mary is startled by the vision of the angel, she is more so by the message he proclaims: "Do not be afraid, Mary, for you have found favor with God. And behold, you will conceive in your womb and bear a Son, and you shall name him Jesus."

"How can this be," we can hear Mary asking the angel, "since I have no relations with a man?" She had promised God to remain a virgin; was God asking her through the angel to do otherwise? Gabriel answered Mary quickly, reassuring her that the gift of her virginity to God would remain untarnished: "The holy Spirit will come upon you, and the power of the Most High will overshadow you. Therefore the child to be born will be called holy, the Son of God."

Overwhelmed by the news given to her by Gabriel, Mary, a woman of deep faith, utters her fiat: "Behold, I am the handmaid of the Lord. May it be done to me according to your word." Her fiat, spoken softly in a humble home in the village of Nazareth, changed the course of history forever. Through her simple utterance, God's plans begin to unfold. The Son of God descends into the womb of Mary, uniting heaven and earth. At that precise moment, the Holy Spirit, through its mysterious power, accomplishes God's Incarnation: the Word is made flesh and dwells among us. Nothing will ever be the same.

Rejoice, O Mary, through whom joy shall shine forth;
Rejoice, O Virgin, through whom the curse shall be blotted out.
Rejoice, O Mary, the Restoration of the fallen Adam;
Rejoice, O Virgin, the Redemption of the tears of Eve.
Rejoice, O Mary, height hard to climb for human minds;
Rejoice, O Virgin, depth hard to explore even for the eyes of angels.
Rejoice, O Mary, you are the throne of the King;
Rejoice, O Virgin, for you sustain the Sustainer of all.
Rejoice, O Mary, the star that causes the sun to appear;
Rejoice, O Virgin, womb of the divine Incarnation.
Rejoice, O Mary, through whom creation is renewed;
Rejoice, O Virgin, through whom the Creator became a babe.
Rejoice, you, unwedded Bride.
> AKATHIST HYMN

The O Antiphons

O wisdom from the Father's Mouth,
The Word of his eternal love,
Beneath whose firm yet gentle sway
This world is governed from above.
O come! O come!
And teach us all
The ways that lead to life.
> MAGNIFICAT ANTIPHON FOR DECEMBER 17

𝐁eginning December 17, our sense of Advent expectation intensifying, our longing for the Redeemer finds perfect expression in the so-called O Antiphons, which are solemnly sung each evening at vespers in all monasteries until December 23. These seven antiphons are known as the O Antiphons because each starts with the vocative O: "O Wisdom," "O Adonai," "O Root of Jesse," "O Key of David," "O Daystar," "O King of All People," "O Emmanuel."

The O Antiphons, written and sung in the second Gregorian mode of the chant, were all composed according to the same formula in the original Latin. Each begins with an invocation to the Lord that expresses his attributes or messianic titles, then culminates with a longing call and prayer or concrete petition: "O come! And set us free, delay no longer in your love." The exquisite Gregorian melody, which is the same for the seven O Antiphons, expresses beautifully the meaning of the texts, with all of their rich complexity and movement.

The arrival of the beautiful O Antiphons is enthusiastically awaited each Advent in every monastery and sung with the utmost reverence and solemnity. Usually the antiphon is first intoned by the abbot or superior of the monastery, who is attended by two monks bearing candles as in the most solemn occasions. Then all the monks

join in while the altar is incensed and the monastery bells ring in sounds of joy and praise during the antiphon and the Magnificat. It is the highlight of the evening liturgical prayer of vespers, and those who experience it even once never forget it.

A few years ago, while doing some research into the origins of these ancient antiphons in the monastic Office, I found that they were already known in Rome in the second half of the sixth century, during the time that Advent was being elaborated there as a liturgical season. However, it could well be that these antiphons date to an even earlier time, that of the Gallican Rite, such as it was practiced in the south of France and northern Spain. For Advent as a liturgical season was indeed created in France, then Gaul, within the Gallican Rite. There are traces of these antiphons in a poem written in Gaul around AD 750, and they are certainly found in the early antiphonary of Saint Corneille de Compiegne, composed between AD 860 and 880. The first manuscript in which one finds all of them together and which remains in use to this day comes from the ancient abbey of Saint Gall in Switzerland, the manuscript dating back to the year 1000.

These beautiful, evocative antiphons, sung according to the purest lines of the Gregorian chant, create a particular climate of serenity and intense peace in the monk's heart during the last days of our Advent journey, just as Christmas approaches. This monastic climate of serenity opens wide the doors of the heart to the silence and joys of prayer and contemplation. In the depths of our hearts we know with certainty that Christ is coming. He is our Savior, and thus we long for him with inexpressible desire. As evening falls over the universe during the singing of vespers and day gives place to the darkness of night, one is filled with hope and increased yearning for the arrival of the Light that will shine on Christmas Day.

O Sapientia (O Wisdom) (DECEMBER 17)

O Wisdom, O holy Word of God's mouth,
You govern all creation with your strong yet tender care.
Come, and teach us all the ways that lead to life.

VESPERS FOR THE DAY

𝒯he cold December chill permeates the quiet of the monastery. It is the kind of chill that sometimes seeps into our very bones. One longs for the warmth of a cozy fireplace, for the comfort that heat can give. It is the hour of vespers, and the bells are ringing with special solemnity. Starting today, the monasteries around the world make their solemn entrance into the last week of preparation before Christmas. The text of the lovely Advent vespers hymn, Conditor Atmae Siderum, changes to Verbum Salutis, and more importantly, the first of the great O Antiphons, O Sapienta (O Wisdom), begins to be sung at the time of the Magnificat. These beautiful antiphons, pregnant with meaning, are bearers of Advent hope and joy. In them, according to a French liturgist, the Liturgy of Advent finds its fullness and plenitude.

Previously, in another book, I have written about the O Antiphons and their significance in the monastic liturgy. Here, I simply wish to dwell on the rich spiritual content of the antiphon of the day, which opens:

O Wisdom, O holy Word of God's mouth.

The wisdom we call forth is the word of God. The word, according to Saint John, has existed from the beginning in God's bosom. "In the beginning was the word, and the word was with God, and the word was God," he writes. The antiphon takes us to that moment before time began, to the Father's eternal engendering of the Son, of he who has "gone forth from the mouth of the Most High." Here, at vespers, our evening celebration in song, we sing of that first night before the world was created, when the word came forth from the mouth of the Father, full of splendor and majesty.

You govern all creation with your strong yet tender care.

Saint Paul tells us in his Letter to the Colossians that, "In him were all things created in heaven and on earth, visible and invisible." God is the Creator, and Jesus, his eternal Son, is the Lord and master of this created universe. The universe was created for him, who in turn would  come one day to redeem it. This universe, and all of us within it, he tends to with loving care. In the words of the Scriptures, "He orders all things mightily and sweetly."

Come; and teach us all the ways that lead to life.

This *Veni* of the antiphon is the pleading of our Advent journey. All along the days of Advent we have been praying, "Come, Lord Jesus, come." Now, in these solemn final days, we intensify our cry and plea for redemption. Once more we beg him to come and teach us the ways that lead to life eternal.

O Adonai (O Lord of Israel) (DECEMBER 18)

O Lord and Giver of the Law on Sinai,
The Leader of your chosen people Israel,
Appearing in the burning bush,
Revealed to Moses face to face,
O come, stretch out your mighty arms to set us free.
Vespers of the Day

As we journey during these last of our Advent days, we begin to feel more and more the exhilaration of knowing ourselves close to the arrival point. The majestic O Antiphons—full of poetic, symbolic richness—nurture our faith and expectation. They are our daily food on these last days, as we continue to climb the mountain of the Lord.

O Lord and Giver of the Law on Sinai.

Today we call forth the Savior with the invocation *O Adonai*, which in Hebrew translates to *El Shaddai*, the God who reveals himself to Moses on the mountain of Sinai. He is the God of the covenant and the ruler of the house of Israel. In contrast to those who may wish to deny the divinity of Christ, the faith of the Church stands firm on its belief by calling the Savior with the name applied only to God in the Old Testament. The Church is telling us that Jesus, the Messiah we await is, in the words of the Creed, "the only Begotten Son of God, born of the Father before all ages, God from God, Light from Light, true God from true God." With deep humility, we hold on to the ancient faith of the Church. Today, as in ages past, there will be those who contest it and wish to change it. There is no point in arguing with them, for their minds are made up and their beliefs are already elsewhere. As Jesus said to the Samaritan woman, "If you only knew the gift from God." Our faith is this gift from God, the faith preserved in the Church that reveals Jesus as the Son of God.

Appearing in the burning bush, revealed to Moses face to face.

After the Passover, the Lord leads his Chosen People through the desert for forty days and forty nights. It is after that long, arduous, and excruciating journey that God reveals himself to Moses in the burning bush. He not only reveals himself, but he also reveals his name. Like the Chosen People, we, too, are called to traverse the desert during our Advent journey, attempting to reach the mountain of the Lord where he will reveal his name to us. The only difference now is that the name is a new one: Emmanuel. It is a new name to signify that he is about to forge a new covenant with his people.

O Come, stretch out your mighty arms to set us free.

In the old covenant, the great sign of God's love for his people was made visible in their deliverance from Egypt and his leading them into the Promised Land. In the new covenant, his great love for us is not only manifested in his Incarnation and birth, which we are about to commemorate, but even more so during later years in Calvary when he "stretches out his mighty arms" on a wooden cross to save us. It is then that our true deliverance takes place, that our eternal freedom is gained.

O Adonai, *faithful Shepherd of Israel,*
Come to us tonight during evening prayer
As we invoke your holy name.
Come and show us your face,
A face full of tenderness and love.

O Radix Jesse (O Root of Jesse) (DECEMBER 19)

O Root of Jesse, sign of peace,
Before whom all nations stand in awe;
Kings stand silent in your presence;
The nations bow down in worship before You.
O come, and set us free;
Delay no longer in your love.
    Vespers of the Day

The days grow progressively shorter at this time of the year, and a great darkness descends and unfolds upon our universe. Today's vespers, our evening prayer of praise, presents us with another beautiful image of he who is to come: *O Radix Jesse* ("O Root of Jesse," or, in another translation, "O Flower of Jesse's Stem.") The prophet Isaiah once foresaw the destruction of Judah and the Kingdom of David. The only remnant, Isaiah asserts, would be a humble root, a root from Jesse's stem: David's father. It is this humble root that would salvage the lineage of David. From the stem of this root the Savior will bud and flower. The words of one of our Christmas carols expresses this tenderly:

Behold, a rose of Judah, from tender branch has sprung!
A rose from root of Jesse, as prophets long had sung.
It bore a flower bright
That blossomed in the winter
When half-spent was the night.

The rose of royal beauty of which Isaiah sings
Is Mary, maiden Mother, and Christ the flower she brings.
By God's unique design,
Remaining still a virgin,
She bore her Child divine.

The root of Jesse, in the words of the antiphon, is a sign of peace for all peoples. Jesus, our Emmanuel, is sent by the Father to seal this new alliance of peace and reconciliation between the world and God. Colossians 1:19–20 expresses this precisely:

For in him all the fullness was pleased to dwell,
and through him to reconcile all things for him,
making peace by the blood of his cross
(through him), whether those on earth or those in heaven.

Jesus is the *Rex pacificus*, "the Prince of Peace," "whose face the whole world longs to see," as the very first antiphon of Christmas vespers addresses him. As he arrives on Christmas Day, small and humble, yet clothed in eternal splendor, *Tu splendor Patris*, all nations stand in awe. The world has never seen a similar event!

Kings stand silent in your presence;
the nations bow down in worship before you.

This part of the antiphon not only anticipates Christmas but already gives us a glimpse into the Solemnity of the Epiphany, when God's glory will be manifested to the gentiles. The Magi kings, seeing this glory shining in a little child, stand dumbstruck in his presence, rapt with wonder and awe. As the Magi, we, too, can only be silent before the great mystery. In our deep silence, we offer him our humble worship.

O come, and set us free; delay no longer in your love.

The phrase *Veni ad liberandum nos*, or "Come and save us," has been the cry of our hearts all along the Advent journey. Now that we see this salvation arriving, so close at hand, we add, *Jam noli tardare:* "Hurry, Lord, do not tarry in your love for us, delay no longer in your coming."

O Clavis David (O Key of David) (DECEMBER 20)

O Key of David and Power of the house of Israel,
What you unlock, no man can close,
For you alone can bind fast.
O come, break down the prison walls of death
For those who dwell in darkness
And the shadow of death.

VESPERS OF THE DAY

The calendar tells us that tomorrow is officially the first day of winter (some years, it's December 22). Our evening, an otherwise gloomy and frosty one, is tempered by the many lights in our chapel and the warmth they impart. The solemnity of these last days of Advent is expressed by the many candles burning at vespers, including the oil lamps in front of our many icons, the incense used at the Lucernarium and the Magnificat, and the bells ringing joyously during the singing of the great O Antiphons and the Magnificat. The beauty of the Offices and the chant, the light and warmth from our candles, the sweet scent of the incense, the lovely sound of the bells: all of this changes what would usually be an ordinary winter evening into an expectant, festive nocturnal moment.

O Key of David and Power of the House of Israel.

These are the ancient messianic titles used by the Prophets to foretell the coming of the Messiah and designate his role. When Christ, the king of David, arrives, he will unlock and reveal all the secrets and mysteries of the old covenant. In him shall all the prophecies be fulfilled. In the new dispensation and covenant, he is head of a new Israel: the Church. He is the leader of this body, the Church, to which we all belong. Therefore, he has power and dominion over us all.

What you unlock, no man can close, for you alone can bind fast.

Christ, the Messiah, the Key of David, comes to unlock for all, Jews and gentiles alike, the doors of the kingdom of God. He alone possesses the keys, and it will be he who invites all, be they just or sinners, into his eternal banquet. No one shall be excluded. This is precisely the good news of the gospel he will proclaim one day.

O come, break down the prison walls of death, for those who dwell in darkness and the shadow of death.

This is the fervent prayer of the expectant house of Israel, the cry for its liberation. In Psalm 44 we find an echo of this sentiment, which we, in turn, make our own:

Awake, O Lord, why do you sleep?
Arise, do not reject us forever!
Why do you hide your face
And forget our oppression and misery?
For we are brought down low to the dust,
Our body lies prostrate on the earth.
Stand up and come to our help!
Redeem us because of your love.

O Oriens (O Daystar) (DECEMBER 21)

O Daystar, splendor of eternal light
And Sun of Justice,
O come, shine on those who dwell in darkness
And the shadow of death.

VESPERS OF THE DAY

*T*oday, in our hemisphere, the calendar marks the winter solstice. It is therefore the shortest day of the year. After the solstice, beginning on December 22, daylight slowly begins to lengthen. Similarly, we are at the point of our Advent journey in which we see the Light approaching at a close distance, the true Light who will shine on Christmas Day. This is the Light we have been seeking and have yearned for during the journey, the Light that will finally dispel all darkness from our hearts.

O Daystar, splendor of eternal light and Sun of Justice.

The Latin *O Oriens* is translated in several different ways: O Daystar; O Dayspring; O Radiant Dawn. Each of these is rich in

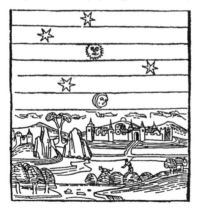

meaning and symbolic significance. In the early days of the Church, the first Christian temples were constructed looking toward the east, the Orient, from where Christ came and was expected to return. Our own oratory chapel is built that way, so that we can pray looking toward the east. The sun, a symbol of Christ, rises daily from the east. And from the sun, high in the heavens, comes light and life. Similarly it is from Christ, the Sun of Justice, that we Christians receive light and life. Christ, the Oriens from on high, is the Light of the World, and it is ultimately in his light that we shall one day see the radiance and splendor of the Father. "He who sees me sees the Father," proclaims Jesus. As we sing daily at vespers in the *Phos Hilaron*:

O gladsome light
Of the holy glory of the Immortal Father;
Heavenly, holy, blessed Jesus Christ.

O come, shine on those who dwell in darkness
and the shadow of death.

It is because we are in darkness, the darkness of our confession and helplessness, that we recognize our instinctual need for light and salvation. Sinners that we all are, we recognize the deadly effects of sin in our lives. We know ourselves indeed sitting in a depressed, desperate state, under the "shadows of darkness and death." Christ alone can liberate us from these shadows. Fortunately for us, we know of his great love and compassion, his unbroken promise to come to us as our Savior.

In the tender Compassion of our God
The dawn from on height shall break upon us,
To shine on those who dwell in darkness and the shadow of death
And to guide our feet into the way of peace.
Or consider the words of an old German hymn we sing daily:

Long is our winter, dark is our night;
Come, set us free, O saving Light!

O Rex Gentium (O King of All People) (DECEMBER 22)

O King of all nations,
The desired One of their hearts,
The cornerstone that joins in one
The people's sin had kept apart.
O come, and save the creature
You once formed from earth and dust.

<small>VESPERS OF THE DAY</small>

I hold to the view that to benefit spiritually, at a deeper level, from the great O Antiphons, one has to learn to sing them in their original melody, either in Latin or in English. Fortunately there are wonderful and precise adaptations of English texts to the Gregorian melody. We know that in the Gregorian chant, the words and music are so tied together that to distill, syllable by syllable, the meaning of the words, we must make every effort to sing them. The exquisite Gregorian melody, used for all the seven O Antiphons, is written in the same second mode, the "D mode," expressing beautifully the richness of the texts in all their evocation and complexity. This soul-stirring melody, one of the purest of the Gregorian repertoire, creates a soothing, healing, and serene effect in all those who sing or listen to it. The antiphons are a source of pure joy. For those who sing them, they become semi-sacramental, flowing like rivers through the body and mind, carrying us away in their currents. As the psalmist says, "It is good to give thanks to the LORD, to make music to his name, O Most High" (Psalm 92).

Those who cannot sing the antiphons in their original Gregorian melody can still use the text and sing them to the tune of *O Come, O Come, Emmanuel.* This is very practical for home use around the table, at dinner time. Those who cannot sing at all can pray it, listening if they can to a recorded rendition of the antiphons. Many of the Gregorian chant compact discs carry it.

O King of all nations, the Desired One of their hearts.

In the preceding O Antiphons, our point of reference was the Jewish Old Testament, using the messianic titles the Israelites applied to the expectant Messiah. Starting today, our horizon enlarges to encompass all peoples. The Messiah, the Savior sent by God, comes to be king not only of the Chosen People, but of all peoples, including the gentile nations. As a matter of fact, a literal translation of *O Rex Gentium* would read, "O king of the gentiles." God, in his great love, calls all his children of the earth to salvation. He offers them, Jews and gentiles alike, a Savior. Jesus is sent by the Father into the world to unite all peoples and be king of all. In the words of Saint Paul, "There is neither Jew nor Greek, there is neither slave nor free person, there is neither male nor female; for you are all one in Christ Jesus" (Galatians 3:28).

The people's great longing for his coming, therefore, is not surprising. He is the "Desired One" of their hearts, for he is the one who has come to free them from their previous captivity. He is the one who comes to bring unity to all of his people.

The cornerstone that joins in one the people's sin had kept apart.

Jesus, in Matthew 21:42, calls himself the cornerstone, the foundation upon which his Church will be built. It is in this Church, his body, that he will gather all people into one. Those of all languages and nationalities, races and backgrounds, will finally find their true home in the one Church of God, whose cornerstone is Christ himself.

O come, and save the creature you once formed
from earth and dust.

Our Advent cry for help, "O come," is again heard at the completion of the antiphon. "O come, and save the creature you once formed from the dust" is our plea to God's pity and love. We pray and never cease praying. Whether we need something or not, prayer is our one direct recourse to God. As a great saint once said, "Prayer is the one thing that touches the heart of God." In these last days of Advent we keep vigil in constant prayer that we may worthily receive the gift from on high: Christ, our Savior.

O Emmanuel (DECEMBER 23)

O Emmanuel, our King and Lawgiver,
The long-awaited hope of the nations,
Savior of all people;
O come, our Lord and God,
Set free the people whom You love.
    VESPERS OF THE DAY

*N*ow that our Advent journey is about to draw to a close, we turn our thoughts to Bethlehem. In spirit, we travel to that faraway place, where the great mystery is to be unveiled in a humble babe. A poignant Byzantine liturgical text tells us:

Now that the time of our salvation draws near...prepare yourself, O Bethlehem, for the birth. Receive the Mother of God: for she comes to you to give birth to the Light that never sets...Let everything that has breath praise the Maker of all!

Tonight we praise the Lord with the last of our Advent vespers. The final of the great O Antiphons is sung. Already at lauds, during our morning praise, the liturgy forecasting the news told us to ready ourselves: *Ecce completa sunt*, is proclaimed, or "Behold, all things are accomplished" which were spoken by the angel concerning the Virgin Mary. As the bells ring during the singing of the last great O Antiphon and the Magnificat, we draw deeply into ourselves once more, knowing now with certainty that the prophecies of long ago are soon to be fulfilled. The promised one is at the doors, ready to knock upon them.

O Emmanuel, our King and Lawgiver,
the long-awaited hope of nations.

For the first time today we call upon him who is coming with the name given to him by the angel: Emmanuel, meaning, "God is with us." We recall also the words of the prophet Isaiah: "The young woman, pregnant and about to bear a son, shall name him Emmanuel." The very meaning of the name reveals to us the depth and tenderness of God's love for us. True lover that he is, he waits to be with us. He wants to be one of us, to dwell and remain with us always. He desires to share our human nature, and he wants us to share his divine life. Indeed, he is the "lover of humankind," as the Eastern Liturgy frequently calls him. With his coming in the flesh among us, we stand in awe as "the grace of God has appeared, saving all" (Titus 2:11). The long-awaited hope of all nations is soon to be rewarded and fulfilled.

O come, our Lord and God, set free the people whom you love.

This last *Veni*, the final "O come," summarizes our Advent journey: its prayer, longing, and constant yearning for salvation. Come, Lord, set free the people whom you love. This last verse of the antiphon gives us the necessary incentive we need for the last miles of our journey. A little bit longer, and then tomorrow his glory shall be revealed to us!

Christmas

In Bethlehem in a manger of dumb beasts,
From a virgin now is born a young child
Who is the pre-eternal God.
O what a wonder is this!
BYZANTINE MATINS OF THE FOREFEAST OF THE NATIVITY

*T*his simple, short text from the Byzantine Office expresses to us concretely the mystery we celebrate on Christmas Day and throughout the length of this particularly liturgical season. First of all, the text is an affirmation, without a trace of doubt, of the fact of the Incarnation. For the "young child" is also "the pre-eternal God," and he is "from a virgin now born." Mary gave flesh to the Word, and so Christmas in a unique way is also a feast of the Mother of God.

The text also tells us that Jesus, the Son of God and son of Mary, is born "in Bethlehem" in the company and "manger of dumb beasts." In those days, Bethlehem was a small, forsaken village, despised by the great of the world. Thus, from the very beginning of his appearance into this world, Jesus, the Son of the Most High, embraces a state of lowliness and casts his lot among the poor, the destitute, the forgotten and undesirables of this world. The first ones to receive the good news of the birth of the Savior were the humble, poor shepherds of the surrounding region, who were taking turns "keeping the night watch over their flock" (Luke 2:8). To them the angel of the Lord said, "Do not be afraid; for behold, I proclaim to you good news of great joy that will be for all the people. For today in the city of David a savior has been born for you who is Messiah and Lord. And this will be a sign for you: you will find an infant wrapped in swaddling clothes and lying in a manger" (Luke 2:10–12).

Thus, the humble shepherds and the dumb beasts were among the first, together with Mary and Joseph, to offer homage and adoration to the little child lying in the manger, their Lord and God. "O what a wonder is this." And what a lesson it contains for us all! From the moment of his birth to the moment of his death, Jesus deliberately and clearly shows us where his preference lies and the way that we, his disciples, must follow.

As we celebrate once more this beautiful feast of the Incarnation, let us pray for the grace to learn the admirable lessons the Lord wishes to teach us through the example of his holy birth. May our Lady, Saint Joseph, and the humble shepherds inspire in us the courage to follow the Lord Jesus faithfully in his self-emptying and in his preference for the poor and lowly, even though it may seem today as it was then, so contrary to the values of the world.

Today Christ is born!
Today the Savior has appeared.
Today the angels sing on earth,
And the archangels rejoice.
Today the just exult, saying:
Glory to the Lord in the highest.
Alleluia.

MAGNIFICAT ANTIPHON FOR
CHRISTMAS DAY

The Holy Family

The child's father and mother were amazed at what was said about him.
LUKE 2:33

One of the lovely customs of the season, at homes or in the monastery, is to prepare the crèche just before Christmas Day itself. In the monastery, we actually set up the Nativity scene in several important places: the church, the refectory, the library, and the common room. Obviously the most important one is the crèche prepared for the church, which receives a blessing just before Midnight Mass.

The Nativity set used in the church is very stark in its simplicity. Many years ago, while we were building the chapel, someone made us the beautiful gift of this Nativity set. It comes from the Philippines, and the figures are made of a dark, handsome wood proper to the place. Unlike other Nativity sets, which sometimes are elaborate with multiple figures, this one is plain and simple. It only has four figures: the Baby Jesus, Mary, Joseph, and an angel. It depicts the Holy Family, and nothing else.

The Infant Jesus, small as he is, is the center of the crèche. He is the reason for the celebration of Christmas. Mary and Joseph turn toward him. All things look to the small, silent Infant, and find in his little smile an expression of God's tenderness for his people. The grace of God that brings salvation appears in his little person, and radiates from him for all people to see.

Through this humble crèche, Jesus is present in our midst, telling each one of us, "See how much I love you." In the crèche, he awaits patiently our visit. He wishes to see us, so that we can share with him everything that is happening in our lives. As we draw close to him, we hear his welcome to each of us: "Peace be to you."

In the humble crèche, Jesus introduces us to the two figures close to him, the two persons he loves the most on earth, and the ones who also love him the most: Mary, his mother, and Joseph, his stepfather. Now that we meet them, and are accepted into such a privileged company, we make ourselves at home in the crèche, and like the ancient shepherds, keep company to the tiny Infant with Mary and Joseph, and also with the angel. We are stunned at the great mystery before our eyes, and we plunge ourselves into silent adoration of the Word made flesh.

The humble crèche of Bethlehem is truly a place where we can all learn to discover Christ and find out who he really is. In the silence of the crèche, with Mary and Joseph by our side, we begin to learn the first lessons of the gospel. There is no other substitute for such an experience.

Solemnity of the Mother of God (JANUARY 1)

Holy Mother of God, save us.
BYZANTINE PRAYER

$\mathcal{J}$n the very first Christian centuries, the early Christians honored Mary, the Mother of Jesus. The gospels describe the highly eminent role assigned to Mary in the unfolding mystery of our salvation. Mary is present from the very beginning, from the moment of the conception and birth of the Savior, and she is also present at the end, at the foot of the cross.

Among all the titles ascribed to Mary throughout the ages, the most significant one was given to her by the early Christian Church, united in solemn council at Ephesus in 431. There, moved by the Holy Spirit, the Church of God proclaimed her to be the *Theotokos*, the "God-bearer," that is to say, the Mother of God. The Mother of

God is proclaimed to be an integral part of the mystery of Jesus Christ, the mystery that was in God's mind before the ages began.

The mystery of the Mother of God, embedded within the depths of the mystery of Christ himself, is therefore very dear and very sacred to the Christian faithful but ever beyond their comprehension. In most icons of the Mother of God, she is portrayed carrying the Christ Child in her arms. There we see that while the eyes of Jesus rest lovingly upon his mother, her gaze is directed tenderly toward us and toward all those who approach him. She shows her Son to each of us, silently saying, "Behold your God and your Savior."

In the gospels, as in the icon, the Mother of God is always portrayed in physical proximity to Jesus and is always pointing to him. In the Magnificat, her song of praise, she calls herself "God's lowly handmaid," showing us the depths of her self-effacing attitude before the immense mystery of Jesus Christ. She is only the humble creature who bore him, the Son of God. It is God alone who has done great things in her. It is therefore to him alone, Mary would tell us, that all our adoration, our praise, and our worship belong. It is to him alone that our obedience and the undivided attention of our hearts must be given.

As we are allowed to enter with the eyes of faith into the mystery of Christ, we rejoice with great joy as we discover that Mary is both the Mother of God and also our mother. She has engendered us at the foot of the cross when Jesus said to her, "Woman, behold, your son" (John 19:26). As Jesus commits the beloved disciple John to the maternal care of his mother, so does he also entrust us to her. In the person of John, it is all of us who become children of Mary.

The presence of the Mother of God in our lives is then very real. She is our mother, our friend, our helper, our refuge in time of danger, and consolation in time of affliction. She is our luminous guide when we lie in darkness and in the midst of despair. On our journey toward God's kingdom, her warm presence dispels our sense of loneliness. She gives us the strength and courage needed for the journey. We walk, but never alone, for the Mother of God is always with us. If we remain quiet and don't interfere or fuss too much about ourselves, we should be able to feel her consoling presence as we pray the ancient prayer:

We entrust ourselves to your protection,
Holy Mother of God.
Listen to our prayers,
help us in our daily needs,
And save us from every danger,
O glorious and blessed Virgin.

Sub Tuum Praesidium, Fourth Century Coptic Prayer

Epiphany of the Lord

All you who seek the gentle Christ,
To heaven lift your eyes and see
The sign of glory without end,
Revealing his descent to earth.

This gleaming star outshines by far
The brightness of the sun's full glow,
For it declares that God made man
Has come to bless and save us all.

He is the king of nations all,
Expected by the Jews of old,
The promised seed of Abraham,
Born of his race in course of time.

All glory, Jesus, be to you,
Revealed to all the nations now,
To God the Father glory be
And to the Spirit endlessly. Amen.

PRUDENTIUS, "QUICUMQUE CHRISTUM" EPIPHANY HYMN FOR LAUDS

*A*s we reach the beautiful feast of the Epiphany of the Lord, the twelve joyful days of Christmastime in the monastery come to a close. In ancient times the feast was called Theophany, and it was celebrated on Christmas Day itself. In the fourth century, Pope Julius I made two different feast days out of the original one. Christmas remained fixed on December 25, and Epiphany was moved to January 6, twelve days afterward.

Epiphany means "manifestation," and in the Christian East is still celebrated under its original name, *Theophany*, "manifestation of God." In the Latin Mediterranian countries, the feast was commonly known as *Festum Trium Regem*, "Feast of the Three Kings." In the English-speaking countries, it was known as the Twelfth Day of Christmas. Epiphany is also often referred to as the Feast of Lights, the name taken from the beautiful passage from the prophet Isaiah (60:1–3, 19) read both during the Office of Matin and again later at Mass:

Arise! Shine, for your light has come,
the glory of the LORD has dawned upon you.
Though darkness covers the earth,
and thick clouds, the peoples,
Upon you the LORD will dawn,
and over you his glory will be seen.
Nations shall walk by your light,
kings by the radiance of your dawning....

No longer shall the sun
Be your light by day,
Nor the brightness of the moon
Give you light by night;
Rather, the LORD will be your light forever,
Your God will be your glory.

The feasts of Christmas and Epiphany celebrate the mystery of the Incarnation of Christ, God made as man. And Christ is the Light of the World, which is why the rich symbolism of light, especially during our long, dark winter days, is particularly cherished by all those who celebrate the feasts. The last antiphon of the first vespers of the solemnity, very expressive in the Gregorian Chant, proclaims, "This wondrous star shines like a flame, and points out God, the King of Kings. The Wise Men saw it and offered their gifts to the great King."

There are many monastic customs varying from country to country and from monastery to monastery, associated with the feast of the Epiphany. One beautiful ancient custom that remains alive to this day in almost all monasteries is the solemn announcement during Mass or during the reading of the Martirology of the dates for the movable feasts of the coming year: Ash Wednesday, Easter, Ascension, Pentecost, and, at the end, the first Sunday of Advent. The announcement proclaims, "As we have recently rejoiced over the birth of our Lord Jesus Christ, now through the mercy of God, we can look forward to the happiness that will stem from the resurrection of the same Lord and Savior." With Epiphany we in the monastery reach the peak of our Christmas celebrations. Then the year proceeds seemingly slowly, as winter follows its normal course, and our monastic solitude becomes more complete during the cold months. Not too far on the horizon, however, is the arrival of the Lenten-spring, with its hidden promise of Easter joy.

O Christ, a light transcendent
Shines in thy countenance
And none can tell the sweetness,
The beauty of thy grace.

In this may thy poor servants
Their joy eternal find;
Thou callest them, O rest them,
Thou Lover of mankind.
> JOHN OF DAMASCUS

Candlemas: A Feast of Lights (FEBRUARY 2)

Adorn your bridal chamber, O Sion,
And receive Christ, the King.
Greet Mary, the gate of heaven, with loving salutation;
For she carries the King of glory, the new Light.
In the temple stands the Virgin,
Embracing in her arms the eternal Son
Begotten before the day-star.
The elder Simeon receives him in his arms
And proclaims to the nations:
He is the Lord of life and death,
The Savior of the world.
> *"ADORNA THALAMUN TUUM, SION,"*
> ANTIPHON SUNG DURING THE PROCESSION OF THE FEAST

Forty days after the solemn Christmas festival, on February 2, the churches of the East and West celebrate the beautiful feast of the Presentation of the Lord in the Temple, thus completing the cycle that started with Advent and peaked with Christmas and the Epiphany. This ancient feast originated, as do many of our Western liturgical feasts, in the Christian East, where it was known by its Greek name, the Hypapante, the "Meeting," or the "Encountering." According to Mosaic law, forty days after the birth of a male child, the mother had to present him in the Temple while also making a sacrificial offering of a lamb or two turtledoves. This sacrifice served as purification for the mother after birthing (in the West this feast was sometimes called the Purification of Mary).

Jewish custom also asserted that all first-born creatures, whether human or animal, were to be consecrated in a special way to God. Mary and Joseph were known for always being obedient to all the precepts of Jewish law. Thus, on the appointed day they brought the Infant Jesus to the Temple, where, according to the gospel story, he is received, blessed, and em-braced by the elder Simeon and the righteous prophetess Anna (Luke 2:22–38). They both recognize in the young babe the Savior promised by God long ago to Israel. As they meet him for the first time in the flesh, their joy, which cannot be contained, is expressed in songs of thanksgiving and praise. The significance of the encounter of the elder and the recently born, helpless infant is expressed, I find, in terms of

great tenderness and beauty in the Byzantine texts for the Offices
of the day:

Simeon tells us: Whom do you bear in thine arms,
That you rejoice so greatly in the Temple?
To whom do you cry and shout:
Now I am set free, for I have seen my Savior?
This is he who was born of a Virgin;
This is he, the Word, God of God,
Who for our sakes has taken flesh
To save humankind. Let us worship him!
        Office of Great Vespers

This lovely, deeply touching feast of the Lord—impregnated
with mystery, humility, and tenderness—has been dearly loved
by monks and nuns throughout the ages and celebrated in most
monasteries with great solemnity. First of all, there is the procession
with hymn, antiphons, and candles through the monastic cloister,
as the monks proceed toward the church for Mass. Processions are
important, frequent rituals in monasteries, where they enhance, with
both dignity and recollection, the spirit of the monastic liturgical
celebration. The drama and decorum of monks in procession is
particularly appropriate, I think, for today's feast. The procession
becomes a sort of cortege where the monks, united with Mary and
Joseph, accompany the Lord as he enters the Temple to be offered
to his Father. As the monks walk slowly in procession, we carry in
our hands lighted candles that have just been blessed at the beginning of the rite.

Today's feast is commonly known by its English name, Candle-
mas, for candles play an important role in the liturgy of the day. The
theme of light—based on the evocative words of Simeon, who calls

the Christ Child "a light to enlighten the nations"—permeates the entire liturgy of the feast. Today the Christian Church reaffirms the truth of Simeon's words that Jesus is the true Light of the World by placing the blessed candle in our hands. Thus, we also symbolically receive Christ in our hands and arms as the blessed Simeon and Anna once did long ago.

The fact that candles have such a prominent and central place in today's liturgy is particularly important, I think, for those who follow the monastic way, for candles are in general very expressive of the devotional life of monasteries: there are the four candles of the Advent wreath, the Christmas candle lit on Christmas Day, and the Easter candle lit during the whole of paschaltime. Then there are the everyday candles used during the celebration of the Eucharist and the monastic Offices, the candle that accompanies the Eucharist taken to a sick monk in his cell, and the candles and oil lamps lit in front of our icons, which convey to the Lord, to his holy Mother, and to God's friends the saints our humble homage and the silent petition of our prayers. The dancing yet steady flames of the candles in our chapel speak to me of those intangible realities the monk seeks and at times dimly perceives during his long hours of prayer. The comforting, ethereal aura springing from their light affirms for the monk the reality of a mysterious presence, a presence that can be sensed only with the eyes of faith. Candles are, in a way, messengers of he who is both mystery and the invisible one.

God created the world and he bestowed upon it night and day. We know the sequence of darkness and light. But Christ is the true Light. He came into the world to give us the light that we may believe... and he commanded that our light, as Christians, should shine before men.

MOTHER THEKLA, *EXPRESSIONS OF FAITH*

Saint Basil's Day (JANUARY 2)

Whatever a man may possess over and above what is necessary for life, he is obliged to do good with, according to the command of the Lord, who has bestowed on us the things we possess.

SAINT BASIL THE GREAT, *THE MORALS, I*

One of the first monastic feasts of the New Year is the feast of "our holy father Saint Basil" (January 2), as Saint Benedict lovingly calls him in the holy Rule, acknowledging him to be one of the great fathers of monasticism. Saint Benedict was forever grateful to Saint Basil and to all the earlier fathers and mothers of the monastic tradition, which he in turn would amplify and expand for new generations of monks and nuns in the West.

Saint Basil the Great was born in Cappadocia around 330 and died there in 379. He was born into a remarkable old family of wealth and distinction, in which the grandparents, the parents, the brothers, and the sisters were all numbered among the saints. He received a solid classical education in the schools of Caesarea, Athens, and Constantinople, then settled in the region of Pontus, where he consecrated himself wholeheartedly to the communal form of monastic life. He had a vast influence on the early development of the monastic movement, particularly in the East, where many monks and monasteries still follow the general principles of monastic life he laid down for his disciples. Saint Basil was not only a great monk but also a great bishop and father of the Church, a charismatic man filled with the Holy Spirit, whose writings and wisdom are still a source of nourishment for our spiritual lives today, as they have always been.

Upon entering the secular New Year and often hearing "Happy New Year" being exchanged among friends and family members, the monk pauses to reflect upon the true meaning of a new year. Very often, when someone says, "Happy New Year," the greeting seems to convey the simple idea that we are adding one more stage to the expansion of our lives, and that one hopes it will be a good one from a material point of view. This attitude presents a very shallow picture of life as a succession of years. This is a rather sad and almost fatalistic way of looking at life and at the new year ahead of us.

Some of the greeting cards we receive in the mail speak also of happiness and prosperity for the New Year. While these good wishes are offered to us by friends with deep sincerity, the monk cannot help but reflect on how both happiness and prosperity are at times of a transient or elusive nature. For the monk, entering into a new year is serious business. It gives him the occasion to look deeply into the mystery of time, which in turn reminds him of his own mortality—the years are fleeting and indeed pass by quickly, in no time evaporating into the mystery of eternity. This is why the monk can't help but use the beginning of a new year to remind himself of those intangible realities that are essential for daily living and that no one can take away from us, such as peace, hope, inner growth, and love.

To be at peace with God, with oneself, and with all those one interacts and lives with is a more precious gift than all the wealth of the world assembled. To be anchored in hope—a hope that helps us accept without complaint both the blessings and the sufferings that are found in daily life, a hope that reveals to us each moment the presence of a loving God who is watching over us and standing by our side throughout all of life's circumstances—is a more comforting, fulfilling, and desirable thing than all the empty prosperity the world can offer.

As the new year comes upon us, the monk, in his monastic solitude, prays to the Lord of the universe to grant everyone the gift of peace and the blessing of hope. The prayer does not end there; it continues throughout the rest of the year.

No heaven can come to us unless our hearts
    find rest in today. Take heaven!
No peace lies in the future which is not hidden
    in this present instant. Take Peace!
The gloom of the world is but a shadow.
    Behind it, yet within reach...is Joy.
There is radiance and glory in the darkness, could we but see,
And to see we have only to look;
I beseech you to look.
    FRA GIOVANNI DI CAPISTRANO

Saint Antony the Great, Father of Monks (JANUARY 17)

His face had an extraordinary gracefulness; this too was a gift from the Lord; in fact, if those who didn't know him wanted to single him out when he was among a group of monks, they went toward him without looking at the others, attracted almost as it were by his features. And yet he differed in no way from the others as regards height of build, but only for his perfection of virtue and his purity of spirit.
    SAINT ATHANASIUS, *LIFE OF SAINT ANTONY*

During our long winter solitude, the feast of Saint Antony arrives on January 17. This is appropriate because Antony—the first monk, the Father of Monks—was a hermit and a lover of the solitary life in the desert.

Saint Antony lived in Egypt between 251 and 356. At age eighteen he heard in church the gospel text, "There is still one thing left for you: sell all that you have and distribute it to the poor, and you will have a treasure in heaven. Then come, follow me" (Luke 18:22). Antony, touched by grace, was so moved the moment he heard those words that he instantly decided to leave everything behind and retire to an unapproachable place in the Egyptian wilderness. In the solitude of the desert, Antony strove to center his entire life on God alone. This he did by means of continual prayer, meditation on the word of God, manual work, discipline, and ascetic practices. In his old age, he imparted wisdom to his disciples and encouraged them to remain faithful to God till the end of the monastic life they had chosen. The life of Saint Antony was written by the great church father and champion of the faith Saint Athanasius, who knew Antony personally. This life had such influence in both the East and the West, contributing to the expansion of the monastic ideal in the early Christian centuries and inspiring generations of monks, that Saint Antony is rightly called the Father of Monks.

In our modest monastic chapel, next to the wood stove, hangs an icon of Saint Antony. On special feast days, a small oil lamp is lit in front of the icon during the monastic Offices. There is a certain something in this icon that speaks to me of the transformation by grace of the man Antony into the monk Saint Antony. His presence in our midst, filled with a quiet nobility and inner radiance, seems to convey the truth of his words: "I no longer fear God, but I love him. For love casts out fear" (Saint Antony, Apothegm 32). This love of God, which the humble monk Antony attained to such heights and degrees, continues to be today the sole reason for a Christian monastic life.

Always breathe Christ and trust him.
<small>Saint Antony's last admonition to his disciples</small>

Saint Scholastica, Mother of Nuns (FEBRUARY 10)

Let the Christian people rejoice
in the glory of the gracious virgin, Scholastica;
But most of all, let the choir of virgins and nuns
be glad celebrating the feast of her who,
Pouring forth her tears, entreated the Lord;
And because she loved so much,
she obtained greater power from him.

MAGNIFICAT ANTIPHON OF THE FEAST

During the chilly days of mid-February, when winter at times begins to give us a hint of the forthcoming spring, we celebrate in the monastery the feast of the very quiet and monastic Saint Scholastica (February 10). I call her a quiet saint, for so little is known about her, and the little we know has come to us only indirectly through Pope Gregory the Great's biography of Saint Benedict, her famous brother. Though little is known about her, the portrait that Pope Gregory gives is one of a very human and charming saint who makes the work of love and prayer the operative reasons for her life.

Like her twin brother, Benedict, at a young age Scholastica received from God the call to monastic life. Following in the footsteps of her saintly brother, she entered a monastery of nuns near Monte Cassino where Saint Benedict was the abbot of a monastery of monks. Once a year she was permitted to have a visit with her brother, and they used this occasion to speak not of family matters but, more importantly, to speak of God and their spiritual lives.

During one of those family visits, a most delightful episode took place. Toward evening, after a few hours of visiting with his sister, Saint Benedict was getting ready to return to his monastery; such was the Rule. Scholastica, however, begged him fervently to remain with her. Amazed and bewildered, Benedict refused his sister's request, reminding her of their obedience to the Rule and monastic custom. When Scholastica saw that her petition was of no avail, she laid her head in her hands on the table and prayed with tears in her eyes. A violent storm immediately broke, pouring torrential rain and making Benedict's return to his monastery impossible. At this, Scholastica ceased her praying and, looking at her brother with a smile, said to him, "Go now, brother. Return to your monastery and leave me alone, if you can." Benedict guessed what had occurred and, smiling, reproached his sister, "May God forgive you, my sister. What have you done?" To this Scholastica replied with her usual simplicity, "I begged you to stay, and you would not listen to me, so I made recourse to my Lord in prayer, and he heard me." Accepting the divine will, Benedict acceded to his sister's wishes and remained with her until the following morning, sharing with her the joys of heaven. Gregory, commenting on the episode, said of her, "Greater was her power before the Lord, because greater was her love." After this visit, brother and sister didn't see each other

again, for Scholastica died three days later. She had a premonition of her death but did not wish to make her brother aware of it. Upon learning of her death, Benedict ordered his monks to bury her in the monastery tomb prepared for him. So it was done, acknowledging that neither life nor death could separate these two.

Just as Saint Benedict is acknowledged to be the Father of Monks in the West, so we can also rightly call Saint Scholastica the beloved Mother of Nuns. We know that from the onset of monasticism in the desert there were intrepid women who left behind the allures of the world in order to follow Christ via the monastic way. They contributed greatly to the monastic movement from the start. We learn from the writer Palladius, for instance, that during the early years of the desert movement, there were already twelve monasteries of women in the area around Thebes in Egypt. From some of the early monastic literature comes to us the names of such prominent and courageous women as the two Melanies, Macrina, Alexandra, Thais, Syncletica, Euphrasia, Pelagia, Sarah, Mary of Egypt, Euphrosine, Paula, and Eustochia, along with the many other early nuns who not only emulated their brother monks in fervor but in fact often surpassed them in higher and more virtuous lives. The early monks, although very much men of their time and thus limited, acknowledged the extraordinary quality of these women monastics. Some monks wrote down the lives of the women, such as Mary of Egypt, for the edification of monks to come. As some of these authors came to recognize, it was the monks who were in need of imitating the sanctity and zeal of the early nuns.

The monastic life for us [women] is not in essence a battle but a way of love and faith....For only in so glad a love can we make our senses follow after the spirit; hence it may be that women, who love much and intensely, find the fulfillment in monastic life which they always sought and which now absorbs them wholly.

MOTHER MARIA, *SCEPTRUM REGALE*

CHAPTER 7
Spring Liturgical Cycle

Lent

The Lenten spring has come.
The light of repentance is being offered to us.
Let us enter the season of Lent with joy,
Giving ourselves to spiritual strive, cleansing our soul and body,
Controlling our passions as we limit our food,
And striving to live by the virtues inspired by the Spirit.
Let us persevere in our longing for God
So as to be worthy upon the completion of the forty days
To behold the most solemn passion of Christ,
And to feast with spiritual joy
In the most holy Passover of the Lord.
        BYZANTINE LENTEN OFFICE

At the beginning of chapter 49 of the Rule, Saint Benedict states that "the life of a monk ought always to be a Lenten observance," thus emphasizing that for him Lent is not just one more liturgical season among many, but one that mirrors preeminently what the monk's life should be like at all times. He goes on to say that during Lent the monk should conduct his life with the greatest possible purity, avoiding the faults and negligence of the past. The monk will be able to accomplish this, Saint Benedict tells him, by refraining from sin and devoting himself to prayer with tears, to holy reading, to repentance, and to abstinence. Saint Benedict takes the Lenten observance so seriously that he bids his monks to see it as a program and model for all their monastic life.

Saint Benedict would not understand what Lent has become for so many Christians today, trivialized to a time when we give up candy, cut down on television, or make a yearly confession. I find it sad to see that Lent has become reduced to such a poor shadow of the great significance it had during the first Christian centuries. Perhaps we can rediscover again its true meaning and experience anew its rich reality by incorporating into our lives some of the timeless principles that Saint Benedict proposes to all of us as Lenten practices in the Rule.

The first principle that Saint Benedict mentions, and this should be an obvious one, is "refraining from sin." Lent recalls for us, in

particular, the forty days that Jesus spent in the desert doing battle with Satan, the tempter. Lent should be a time for us, too, to do battle, a time to fight not only the great temptations but, perhaps more importantly, our subtle faults, the seemingly small, habitual sins we consent to every day. Sometimes when we examine our consciences, we tend to look only for grave, serious sins and overlook the small ones that have become so encrusted in our personalities that we no longer recognize them for what they are. Lent is a propitious time to take inventory and a close look at our bare selves, to see the obstacles on our journey to God, things that should be eliminated from our lives. Lent provides us the occasion to work toward making radical changes in ourselves.

The second principle that Saint Benedict proposes is for us to apply ourselves to prayer with tears. During the early days of Lent, the gospel parable of the Pharisee and the publican (Luke 18:9–14) is read to us in church. Jesus teaches that the Pharisee's prayer, filled with arrogance and pride, is not pleasing to God. In contrast, the humble prayer of the publican, a tax collector who recognizes his sinfulness and makes appeal to God's mercy with inner tears, is the kind of prayer that touches God. Our Lenten prayer, like the publican's, ought then to be a humble and tearful prayer of compunction, a prayer of simplicity and trust, not in ourselves, but in the loving kindness and tenderness of our God. This is the only form of prayer that can indeed bring us closer to God.

The third principle that Saint Benedict mentions is holy reading. Lent is a season when the reading of the sacred Scriptures, both the Old and the New Testaments, occupies a most important place in the monk's worship. The monk must not only apply himself to the reading of the Scriptures during his formal hours of prayer, but also make room for continuing its reading at other times and intervals. The monk, just as any other Christian, should develop a continual hunger, almost an addiction, for the word of God, for through the Scriptures the Holy Spirit never ceases to speak to and educate us. As one of the early fathers poignantly said, "In the Scriptures Christ prays, weeps, and speaks directly to us." Lent is this wonderful, particularly well-suited time for reading and listening to the voice of God in his word, thus entering into vital direct contact with him.

The fourth principle that Saint Benedict emphasizes is at the heart of the Christian and, consequently, monastic life. Saint Benedict speaks of repentance. At the threshold of Lent, when placing the ashes on our foreheads, the priest repeats the gospel words, "Repent, and believe in the gospel" (Mark 1:15). Repentance, undertaken with humble sincerity and joy, symbolizes the beginning of a new life and is the necessary requirement for making progress in this new life in Christ. Repentance, the work of the Holy Spirit in the innermost part of our hearts, implies a long, sustained spiritual effort. It is true that conversion and repentance are lifelong tasks, but Lent provides us with an exclusive period to work at it intensely. Lent is indeed "a school of repentance," as Father Schememann beautifully wrote, and we receive it every year as a gift from God, a time to deepen our faith and to reevaluate and change our lives.

The last principle mentioned by Saint Benedict, abstinence from food, long associated with Lent, is not solely a Christian or monastic practice. A well-known practice in non-Christian religions, fasting is also sometimes practiced in secular society for purely medical, dietary, or therapeutic reasons. For the Christian, however, fasting from food bears a special connotation, being rooted in the example of Christ, who fasted forty days and forty nights (Matthew 4:2). Christ used fasting, and encouraged his followers to practice fasting, as a way of learning the self-control and personal restraint we need to keep a humble and wise perspective on our Christian life. Through the painful experience of hunger, we come to the realization of our human limitations and of our utter dependence on God. Fasting is not only a physical activity but primarily a spiritual one. Through it we undergo, during our often tedious Lenten days, a process of self-emptying, or self-dying. This process can be painful and wearying, but when carried out under the guidance of the Holy Spirit, it becomes life-giving and the source of powerful grace in our individual lives. For the Christian, fasting is never disconnected from prayer and concentration on God, for the one concluding lesson that we can all get from fasting is the awareness that it deepens in us, and feeds, a tremendous longing, need, and hunger for God.

Saint Benedict, having artfully mastered the practice of these Lenten observances in the example of his own life, encourages the disciple to do the same in the joy of the Holy Spirit, undertaking his monastic journey toward the feast of Easter with the joy of spiritual desire. Easter, with Christ's resurrection, becomes the fulfillment of all of one's spiritual desires.

Lent is a journey, a pilgrimage! Yet, as we begin it, as we make the first step into the "bright sadness" of Lent, we see—far away—the destination. It is the joy of Easter; it is the entrance into the glory of the Kingdom. And it is the vision, the foretaste of Easter, that make Lent's sadness bright and our Lenten effort a "spiritual spring."

FATHER ALEXANDER SCHEMEMANN, *GREAT LENT*

The Joy of Spiritual Longing

During Lent...let [the monk] withdraw from his body somewhat of food, drink, sleep, speech, merriment, and with the gladness of spiritual desire await holy Easter.

RULE OF SAINT BENEDICT, CHAPTER 49

Often we tend to look at Lent as a negative and sad season, filled with prescriptions for abstaining from food, drink, and entertainment, and we forget that the final goal of our Lenten pilgrimage is a joyful one. Saint Benedict in his Rule affirms that, yes, during Lent we all must learn to practice self-control over our bodily appetites, but he encourages the monk to do this in the joy of the Holy Spirit. From the perspective of Saint Benedict, Lent is never meant to be a negative experience. On the contrary, our Lenten observances, including self denial, are directed to create in us an inner transformation that leads us to deeper communion with God, the source of all life and all joy.

As we walk daily through our Lenten pilgrimage, with its sometimes tedious and fatiguing elements, Saint Benedict invites us to never lose sight of our goal. He encourages the monk to undertake his pilgrimage toward the paschal feast, filled with the joy of spiritual desire. This spiritual desire is fulfilled in us on Easter Sunday, with the bursting of new life in joy, by the power of the resurrection of Christ.

Palm Sunday

Glory and praise, and honor be yours,
Christ our King and Redeemer:
Children in the loveliness of youth,
Called out "Hosanna" to greet you!
    GLORIA LAUS BY THEODULPH D'ORLEANS (D. 821)

Today is Passion Sunday. As we join the Lord into his solemn entrance into Jerusalem, we also enter into a special time: Passiontide. It is the holiest time of the year, the destination of our Lenten pilgrimage. By reliving each event, each moment of our Savior's final week before his death, we become participants in those very events. The Offices of Holy Week allow us to follow, step by step, the historical sequence of Jesus' last days. These liturgical Offices are a great aid in helping us relive the experience of those cruel last hours. They do not portray a theatrical experience, like the movies about Jesus presented on TV; rather, they portray how Christ honestly accomplished his redemptive work. By unfolding before our eyes the mysteries of Christ's suffering, death, and resurrection, in all of their historical details, the liturgy allows us to witness the supreme act of God's love. It is a love that has no equal.

Last evening, while the beautiful hymn *Vexilla Regis* was intoned at vespers, I was instantaneously taken by the sacred drama awaiting us throughout the coming week. The Lenten chant and its hymns, which were such help to our prayer, have now given place to those of Passiontide. The Lenten chant, music, and text served the double purpose of purifying us and of preparing us for what was to come. Now that we have arrived at the very doors of Holy Week, a week totally consecrated to the contemplation of Christ's Death and Resurrection, the chant for Passiontide opens for us the hidden meaning contained in the paschal mystery. The chant, mournfully, builds up its crescendo to help us achieve an inner comprehension of the last events in Christ's life. It reaches its peak on Good Friday, when during the stark presanctified liturgy we sing the whole of the *Christus factus est*. Quietly, but also decidedly, the chant works its way to the point where it leads us to encounter the Lord on the road to Calvary. It compels us to accompany him, with grief and tears of repentance, to his last hour. It is the hour of which he often spoke and awaited anxiously for our sake.

The Bridegroom

Behold, the bridegroom! Come out to meet him!
MATTHEW 25:6

Early on during Lent, we place a very special icon of the Lord on the main lectern in the chapel, on the spot where we usually lay the festal or seasonal icon for veneration. This particular icon goes by different names. Sometimes it is designated by the title the Holy Humility of Christ; other times it is called the icon of the *Kenosis*, that is, the self-emptying of Christ. Most commonly, however, the icon is called simply the Bridegroom.

As it happens, I cherish this icon deeply, for it truly represents the mystery of the passion of the Lord in a profound and unique way. It is the icon that accompanies me on my Lenten pilgrimage, the icon that brings me back to the center when I wander astray by the wayside, as I often do. In looking at Christ, in the solemn moment of his self-emptying, one is stricken by his extreme humility, by the way he endured suffering and torture for our sake. He is truly the Man of Sorrows, the Bridegroom who silently proves his love by laying down his own life for us.

At the beginning of Holy Week, the Bridegroom service is celebrated on the churches of the Byzantine Rite. It is an extremely moving service. The icon of the Bridegroom is solemnly enthroned in the center aisle of the church and the mournful singing begins, reminding us of the trial and death of Christ and his patient endurance throughout. In the words and ritual of the service we relive poignantly the hours of the agony and sacred passion. These are not the sufferings endured by an ordinary man; these are the sufferings endured by the God-Man, in whose person the divine and human natures co-exist. The Bridegroom service is a prelude to the events that are to take place on Holy Thursday, Good Friday, and Holy Saturday. The stanzas of the Bridegroom hymn are so expressive and beautiful, especially when sung. Here are some of them for our own meditation and benefit:

Behold, the Bridegroom comes in the middle of the night.
Happy is that servant whom he shall find watching.
On the contrary, unworthy is he who is careless and not ready.
Let us, then, be vigilant and put aside the works of darkness,
Lest we fall into deep slumber;
For the Lord shall come as a thief in the night.

O Bridegroom, more beautiful than all men,
Having called us to the spiritual Feast of Your Kingdom,
Now clothe us with the right wedding garment.
That being adorned in the garment of your beauty,
We may enter into your bridal chamber as your guests
Shining with glory and joy.

Let us cast aside the works of darkness
And go to meet Christ, the immortal Bridegroom,
Carrying sufficient oil in the vessels of our souls,
Strengthened by prayer and fasting,
Vigilantly let us await the Bridegroom, arriving near,
For the bridal chamber is ready, and the wedding Feast is at hand.
Let us love the Bridegroom
By readying our lamps, shining with virtues and deep faith,
That like the wise virgins of the Lord well-prepared,
We may enter with Christ into the wedding Feast
And receive from the Bridegroom the wedding garment,
So that God may grant us an incorruptible crown.

Holy Thursday

Come, O you faithful,
With uplifted minds let us enjoy
The hospitality of the Lord,
Attending the Banquet of Immortality
Spread in the upper chamber.

BYZANTINE OFFICE, HOLY THURSDAY CANON, 9TH SONG

This morning, at 9 a.m., we began singing the first of the three great Offices of Tenebrae, much later in the day than the customary early-morning hour assigned to these Offices. In a way, these Offices are an official entrance into the sacred Triduum, a stark introduction to the drama we are invited to relive in the next these three days. The Psalms for matins speak poignantly of the sufferings endured by God's servant. They insinuate vividly the dramatic mood of those last days as recounted by the gospels. A peak moment in the Office arrives when Jeremiah's Lamentation is sung in its mournful Gregorian melody. In the Lamentation, we hear the cry of our sinful humanity lamenting the devastation caused by the sins of our forefathers, including our own personal ones. The Lamentations, which we shall continue to sing until our last Tenebrae Office on Holy Saturday, express in their deep and touching simplicity the awesome remorse felt by each of us at the suffering our sins caused to Jesus. In the words of Jeremiah, we can hear the whole of creation groaning, weeping, and downcast by its past actions. Our only response lies in the mystery of repentance, in the profound admission that our sinfulness is at the root of our Redeemer's cruel suffering.

In the evening, the recalling of the Last Supper of the Eucharist is the focal point of our liturgical celebration. As the apostles

once did at that moment, we gather around Christ, our master, to celebrate with him his mystical supper. It is the sacrament of his immense love for all of humankind.

Mindful of Jesus' immense, fathomless love, we strive to approach the sacred banquet in the spirit he bequeathed to his disciples: a spirit of humble and sincere love for our neighbor, a spirit of forgiveness and reconciliation toward all. Imbued with this love we chant at that precise moment the *Ubi Caritas*:

There where is love and fraternal charity,
God is present.
Let us rejoice and be glad in him.
Let us fear the living God and love him.
And with unblemished heart be bound to one another.

Love is the sign of true discipleship, the required garment for entering the Bridal Feast. Love is the supreme lesson of Holy Thursday, the final testament of a dying master. We, as disciples, cherish and hold on to this testament, this new commandment, expressing and repeating it in song during the symbolic washing of the feet: *Mandatum novum do vobis: ut diligatis invicem, sicut dilexi vos, dicit Domini* (A new commandment I have given you: Love one another as I love you).

Good Friday

The whole creation was overwhelmed by fear
When it saw You, O Christ, hanging on the cross.
The sun was darkened and the foundation of the earth was shaken
For all things suffered with the creator of all.
Of your own will you have endured this torment for our sakes.
Therefore, we the faithful glorify your great compassion.
BYZANTINE SERVICE OF THE TWELVE GOSPELS

The monastery bells have been silent since yesterday. They last rung during the Gloria of the Mass, and they will not again be heard until the Gloria of the Easter Vigil. Instead, during these grieving days, we have recourse to a pair of wooden clappers to summon us to prayer and meals. Good Friday is a day of profound mourning. The monastic ambiance is stark and grief-stricken, for we are accompanying the Savior on the way to Calvary and are about to witness his drinking of the cup of suffering to the full. This morning, during the Tenebrae Offices, the psalms related the intensity of Christ's pains, the loneliness of his agony. The Lamentations, in their grave and sorrowful tone, conveyed the indescribable suffering of the God-Man, his heart-rending cry of pain. The grievous torments of the crucified Lord find a ready echo in our poor grateful souls, for it is the burden of our iniquities he bears. It is the price of our redemption he is paying.

As we read the passion account, our souls, in sorrow and repentance, follow each step of the Savior's final hours: the agony and sweating of blood in the garden, the betrayal by Judas, his arrest by the soldiers, the trial before Annas and Caiaphas during the night hours, Peter's fears and denials, the court trial before Pilate, the scourging by the soldiers, the insults by the mob, the carry-

ing of a heavy cross and the encounter with his Mother on the way to Calvary, and, lastly, a very cruel death and burial. Deeply moved at the sight and torments of the sinless Lamb of God, we fall down in adoration before him, the crucified Lord, repeating again and again: "Glory to Your passion, O Christ. Glory to your long-suffering, O Lord!"

After a light refection of bread and water, for today is a black fast-day (no dairy is consumed), we keep vigil by the cross from noon until three o'clock, when we attend the solemn Liturgy of the Pre-sanctified. During the liturgy, we venerate and kiss the cross as we sing: "Before your cross, we bow down in worship, O Master, and your Holy Resurrection, we glorify." Our veneration of the cross expresses our repentance and compassion. Our kiss, in contrast to that of Judas, conveys our love and gratitude to the Savior for his selfless sacrifice:

Christian soul, adore your Bridegroom covered with blood,
And in your kiss give him your entire self!

After the veneration of the cross and the recitation of inter-cessory prayers, we partake of the body of the Lord. It is the very body broken and torn for our salvation. Through this sacramental communion, we share intimately in the passion and death of our Lord and master as we eagerly await the glory of his resurrection. Now that we are nourished for the remainder of the journey, we can continue walking toward our final destination with our eyes fixed on the cross, from where "hangs the salvation of the world." We move on with our journey, but all along he who is both our judge and Savior, Christ crucified, is with us. Our hope lies in the mystery of his passion, for only the passion of Christ can save us.

Late in the evening, after a light collation of vegetable soup and a slice of bread, the only meal of the day, we return to the dark, bare chapel. A lonely candle flickers its flame next to the stand holding the icon of Christ's descent from the cross. It is the only light in the austere setting. As we venerate the icon and kiss the body of the crucified, we recall the affliction of his Mother at that precise moment. As Simeon the Elder once prophesied, a sword had pierced her heart. We watch her standing by the cross, grieving as she receives in her arms the dead body of him who she once bore and nursed as a tiny infant. Can anyone understand the depth of her emotions during those hours, the tragedy of her affliction? We seek to console the Mother of God and join ourselves to her tragic sorrow by singing the mournful lamentations of the *Stabat Mater*. At the end, as we pray, sing, weep, and lament with the *Theotokos*, we witness Joseph of Arimathea taking down Jesus' body from the cross. The spotless dead body is deposed and presented to a sorrowful Mother, while we sing and repeat the old troparion:

The noble Joseph,
When he had taken down Your most pure Body from the tree,
Wrapped it in finen linen and anointed it with spices,
And placed it in a new tomb.
But You rose on the third day, O Lord ,
Granting the world great mercy.

The preparation for the burial is now at hand. The Son's dead body is removed from the mother's arms. Two faithful disciples, Nicodemus and the "noble Joseph," carry their master's body to a new sepulcher. The grieving Mother follows the funeral procession, weeping bitterly, finding no consolation. An ancient tradition of the Christian East tells us that as the Son sees his Mother's breakdown and is unable to bear her sorrow, he whispers in her ear the consoling words:

Do not lament for me, O Mother,
Seeing me buried in the tomb,
The Son whom you once virginally conceived.
I shall rise as God and be glorified,
And shall raise in glory all those
Who partake your sorrow in faith and love.

In an amazing scene, Jesus entrusted us to the care of his Mother, making all of us children of Mary. Now as we accompany her to the tomb, he foretells in that whisper not only his own glorious resurrection, but also the final glorification of all those who shared in her sorrow with faithful and undying love.

Holy Saturday

O my Christ and my life You were placed in a tomb
All the armies of angels were dazzled
And glorified your divine burial.

How can You die, O my life, how can You lie in a tomb?
By your death, You destroyed the power of death
And raised the dead from their tombs.

O King and God of all, we magnify You!
We honor You and bow to your burial
Through which You have saved us from decay.
Dirges of the Burial, Byzantine Daily Worship

A profound stillness reigns throughout the whole monastic enclosure. It is Holy Saturday, a day of mournful silence and of holy rest. It is "the most blessed Sabbath on which Christ sleeps." The icon displayed for our veneration portrays Christ lying in the grave, along with his Mother, the Apostle John, and the holy women standing by, weeping and mourning. With them, we also sit by the tomb and mourn as we pray and sing the last of the Tenebrae Offices. The lovely antiphons make reference to Jesus, who, after a most tormented death, now reposes in the tomb. *In pace in idipsum, dormiam et requiescam* (I sleep and rest in peace). *Caro mea requiescet in spe* (My body shall rest in hope). One of the responsorials recalls the scene described in Matthew 27: "They buried the Lord and sealed the tomb by rolling a large stone in front of it. They stationed soldiers there to guard it...." Our hearts are numbed as we consider that the author of all life, the Creator of all things, is there lying buried like a poor mortal creature. An ancient homily read during the Offices expresses in fitting manner our bewilderment, our painful and confused sentiments:

"Something strange is happening, there is a great silence on earth today, a great silence and stillness. The whole earth keeps silence because the king is asleep. The earth trembled and is still because God has fallen asleep in the flesh and he has raised up all who have slept ever since the world began. God has died in the flesh and hell trembles with fear."

Keeping watch by Christ's tomb, we experience an incredible sentiment of peace. This is not an ordinary burial, another corpse or another sepulcher. This is a life-bearing tomb, containing within its humble self the author and giver of all life. By his death, Christ brought victory over our mortality, and by his holy burial the corruption brought by sin was destroyed. During one of the final responsories of the Office, we join the faithful women who came to anoint the body of the Savior with myrrh and spices. With them, as we continue to mourn and weep, we sing to proclaim:

This is the most blessed Sabbath on which Christ sleeps,
But on the third day he shall rise again.
Therefore, O Lord our God,
We sing to You a hymn, a song to your burial:
By your burial You have opened for us the gates of life,
And by your death You have slain death and hell.
O God, our deliverer, blessed are You!
Byzantine Matins

Easter

This is the day of the Resurrection,
Let us be illumined, O Christian people,
For this is the day of the sacred Passover of the Lord.
Come, and let us drink of the new river,
Not brought forth from a barren stone,
But from the fount of life
That springs forth from the sepulcher of Christ the Lord.
　　Saint John Damascene, "Easter Canon"

For the monk in the monastery of hermitage, as for other Christians at home, the joyful festival of the Resurrection of the Lord follows the Lenten period of prayer, fasting, and quiet introspection. But just as we are about to arrive at the celebration of this glorious festival, we spend the last days of Holy Week at the foot of the cross with our Lady, in mournful remembrance of the pain and suffering that her son Jesus underwent for our sake. These are very quiet days in the monastery, for we carry the heavy burden of grief in our hearts. Good Friday is a day of black fast, where not even dairy products are allowed, and the fare of the monk is reduced to bread and water or other liquids like tea or coffee, after the stark afternoon Liturgy of Christ's passion, we retire to our cells for more prayer, reading, and meditation. At night, before going to rest, we recite compline and sing the *Stabat Mater* in a mournful Gregorian chant melody that recalls Mary's solitude in suffering as she wept for her son at the foot of the cross.

Holy Saturday follows, called "the most blessed Sabbath on which Christ sleeps," by the liturgy. I am particularly fond of Holy Saturday. In a way, it is even quieter than Good Friday, since no liturgy is celebrated, but we share both in the sorrow of the passion and burial of Jesus and in the anticipated joy of the resurrection. An Eastern Byzantine text poignantly conveys the mystery of Holy Saturday:

O happy tomb! Your received within yourself
the Creator and the Author of life.
O strange wonder! He who dwells on high
is sealed beneath the earth with his own consent.

The stillness, the deep silence, and the peace we experience on Holy Saturday, keeping watch by the tomb of Christ, is perhaps the best preparation for the explosive, all-powerful joy of the resurrection. Very often in life, we are likewise led through loss and sorrow to a new phase of peace and understanding that ultimately culminates in deep joy.

At the end of Holy Saturday, very late and in the midst of the darkness of night, the paschal vigil quietly begins with the blessing of the new fire from which the paschal candle is lit. A procession forms, and the monks and the faithful, with lighted candles in their hands, solemnly follow the paschal candle into the dark church. There the *Exultet*, the glorious proclamation of the resurrection of Christ, is announced in song to the whole world. It is a particularly moving moment in the Easter liturgy to hear the haunting Gregorian melody, in perfect unison with the text, proclaim the wonders of God in the resurrection. After the singing of the *Exultet,* the night vigil proceeds with psalms and antiphons sung in between. Following the readings we reach the climax of our Easter Vigil, the solemn celebration of the Eucharist banquet. At the beginning of the Eucharist, the celebrant intones the *Gloria.* As the monks sing the beautiful Gregorian chant from the Mass I *Lux et Origo* of paschaltime, the bells of the monastery peel out in joy, announcing throughout our hills and valleys the glad tidings of the resurrection.

At the end of Mass, our Easter lamb, the youngest of our flock and a symbol of Christ, the immolated Lamb of God, is blessed with the new Easter water, then taken back to the sheepfold. Easter is a feast when all creation rejoices in the resurrection of the Creator of all life, so the animals, the plants, and the flowers of the monastery all partake in this rejoicing.

I am always so glad to see the myriad daffodils on the monastic property bloom in such profusion during Eastertide. After the blessing of the lamb, a long period of thanksgiving and prayer follows, which allows the monk to quietly absorb the great mystery just commemorated. Before we retire for a few hours of rest, each monks receives a bottle of newly blessed Easter water, which he carries into his monastic cell and which will last him until the following Easter.

In the early evening of Easter Sunday, the solemn vespers of the resurrection are sung in the monastery chapel. The vespers begin with the hymn *Ad Coenam Agni Providi*, which I consider one of the most beautiful in the entire Gregorian repertory. After the hymn the exquisite antiphons of the feast with their respective psalms are sung, relating to us once more the biblical details of the Resurrection. Our solemn vespers reaches its climatic point with the proclamation of the gospel account of Jesus' appearance to the disciples on that first Easter evening. First the book of the gospels and the paschal candle, symbols of Christ, are incensed; then the beautiful account is read. A long silence follows the reading. One can feel the immediacy of the Lord's risen presence. Vespers concludes, as it always does, with the solemn singing of the Magnificat, Mary's song of praise to God for his great wonders.

It is of no small significance that the yearly celebration of Lent, Holy Week, and Easter coincides with the arrival of spring. Lent allows us to face all the grim aspects of our life and points us toward the joyful hope of new Easter life. In monasteries, where the Lenten practice of fasting and penance tends to be rather sober in nature, our joy in the resurrection knows no bounds. It is the most thrilling and uplifting experience of the liturgical year. The bells ring with alleluias; the chapel is filled with fresh flowers and bright lights; the chant echoes the joy of Christ's resurrection, as both monks and nuns greet one another with the traditional "Christ is risen" and its reply, "Indeed, he is risen." Spring and Easter are almost synonymous. The new life of spring, such as the flowers springing up in our gardens, is a symbol fully realized in the springing up of divine life in the inner depths of our hearts. The season of spring and the mystery of Easter, celebrated together, bring us from sorrow and death to the affirmation of hope and experience of the renewal of life in our daily existence.

God send us the springtime lamb
minted and tied in thyme
and call us home, and bid us eat
and praise your name
       ANNIE DILLARD, FROM *FEAST DAYS*

The Ascension of the Lord

Christ's resurrection is our hope, and his ascension is our glory. It was with his human nature that Christ entered heaven and sat on God's throne. This, therefore, is the raising and glorification of our human nature. A human being, one of ourselves, is lifted up to the throne of God.
       SAINT AUGUSTINE

After the blissful and much-needed rain of the last two days, this morning I welcomed the dawn with joy. The early light was serene, unspoiled, and perfectly apt for Ascension Day. I am as grateful for the gift of such exquisite light as for the showers of the last few days, which renewed my confidence.

I went to sing lauds this morning, enchanted by the tranquility of the early hour. There is nothing akin to praising the Lord in that deep stillness, when the rest of the world is still asleep. Today's feast is truly majestic, for it concerns the final glorification of our Lord, king, and master. Jesus is returning to the Father, exalted in glory, because of what he endured for our sake. He has fulfilled the Father's plan and now he is being received back into his bosom. All we can do is to lift up our hearts to him, *Sursum corda*, and follow him with our desire.

I think it is Saint Bernard who says that through desire we already possess the object of our longing. The feast of the Ascension also intensifies the realization of our earthly pilgrimage. We are still here on earth, in via, we still have miles to go to reach our destination. But we can be comforted and strengthened by the hope that Christ, our Savior, has reached the end of his earthly pilgrimage, and now is waiting with open arms for us to join him. As he once spoke: I am going to prepare a place for you, so that where I am you may be also.

The Lord ascended into heaven to send the Comforter into the world. The heavens prepared his throne, and the angels marveled at his sight. Today the Father receives in his bosom him who was always with him. The Holy Spirit commands the angels: "Lift up your gates, O you Princes."

O you nations of the earth, clap your hands, For Christ has ascended to the place where he was before time begun.

O Lord, the Cherubim were amazed at your Ascension, They were dazzled as they beheld You, O God, Rising upon the clouds higher than they could rise. We sing a hymn of praise to You: On this day of your glorious Ascension,

We glorify your tender mercy.
O Christ, splendor and glory of the Father,
As we behold your Ascension on the holy mountain,
We sing a hymn to the beauty of your countenance:
We bow down to your sacred passion,
We venerate your Resurrection and glorify your noble Ascension.
O Lord, ascended into glory: Have mercy on us!

O Lord, life-giving Christ, when the apostles saw You
Ascending upon the clouds, a great sadness filled them.
They shed burning tears and exclaimed:
"O dear Master, do not leave us orphans:
We are your servants whom You loved so tenderly,
As You promised send your Holy Spirit to enlighten our souls!"

Lord Jesus Christ, while You lived on earth
You were God inseparable from the Father, yet a real man.
Through your Ascension, You filled your Mother and the apostles
With a joy that surpasses every other joy.
Through their intercession make us worthy of your elect,
For You are all-holy and infinitely merciful.
    BYZANTINE OFFICE, VESPERS STICHERAS OF THE ASCENSION.

Pentecost

O heavenly King, the Comforter, the Spirit of Truth,
Who are everywhere and fill all things,
Treasury of blessings, and Giver of life!
Come and abide in us,
Cleanse us from all our sins,
And save our souls, O Good One!
    BYZANTINE PRAYER TO THE HOLY SPIRIT

The Thursday that follows the fifth Sunday after Easter is the day when monasteries celebrate the feast of the Ascension of the Lord into heaven. Jesus, having fulfilled his earthly mission, went to the Mount of Olives, took leave of his Mother and the disciples, and ascended from there to his Father in heaven. It was his final act on this earth, but it was an act that

opens to us, his followers, endless possibilities, for Jesus did not return to the Father alone. Through the mystery of the Incarnation, Jesus assumed all of humanity into himself, and now all of us are part of him. As the doors of the kingdom of heaven opened wide to receive the triumphant Lord, the whole of redeemed humanity was also being received and accepted by the Father. The feast of the Ascension celebrates not only Jesus' glorification by the Father, but also the Father's acceptance of each one of us. Jesus opens heaven to us, makes it our destination and permanent home, where one day we will also be received into the warm embrace of a loving Father.

While we are celebrating the ascension, the liturgical chants and readings are already making subtle allusions to the Holy Spirit, the Comforter, whom Jesus will send. The ascension in a sense is a necessary prelude to Pentecost.

The Book of Acts recounts the Pentecost event: "When the time for Pentecost was fulfilled, they were all in one place together. And suddenly there came from the sky a noise like a strong driving wind, and it filled the entire house in which they were. Then there appeared to them tongues as of fire, which parted and came to rest on each one of them. And they were all filled with the holy Spirit and began to speak in different tongues, as the Spirit enabled them to proclaim" (Acts 2:1–4).

Pentecost is a time of fruitfulness, of fullness, of completion. The Holy Spirit is being given to us to continue on earth the work Jesus started. At Pentecost the Holy Spirit appears in the forms of wind and fire, two powerful elements of life on our planet. Pentecost takes place at the time of transition from spring to summer. Summer, with its intense mixture of wind and fire, is a symbolic season of the Holy Spirit, who is the life-giver and the maker of all things new. The heat of summer clothes with exuberant colors the flowers in our gardens and gives magnificent texture and taste to our fruits and vegetables. The fire of the Holy Spirit similarly clothes our souls with colors of grace and makes us taste the sweetness of divine life with God.

Monks throughout the ages have had a special affinity and place in their lives for the Holy Spirit. Saint Seraphim of Sarov affirms that "the whole purpose of the Christian life consists in the acquisition of the Holy Spirit." Monks remind themselves daily of the truth of this teaching and try to attune themselves to the whispers of this mysterious presence who dwells within them, who they know to be the Spirit of God. Without him, monks can do nothing, and he alone can bring a personal monastic life out of chaos into a perfectly unified and harmonious whole. The Holy Spirit upholds the life of God deep within each of us, and his power is the force that mysteriously transforms our lives.

If the soul keeps far away from all discourse in words, from all disorder and human disturbance, the Spirit of God will come in to her, and she who was barren will be fruitful.

ABBA POEMAN, *THE SAYINGS OF THE DESERT FATHERS*

Transitus of Saint Benedict (MARCH 21)

We think of Saint Benedict as the ideal monk, as one who lived as the Rule prescribes, and by this means discovered all the riches and excitement known to those who have penetrated to the heart of the Gospel message, that is, a true understanding of what it is to love God, and our neighbor as ourselves.

BASIL CARDINAL HUME, *IN PRAISE OF BENEDICT*

Today we celebrate the holy death of our father, Saint Benedict, his departure to the heavenly Jerusalem. Benedict had received from the Lord the announcement of his death a year in advance—he knew the day and hour. He prepared for the long journey by receiving the sacrament of the Body and Blood of the Lord. Assisted by their monk, Benedict insisted on remaining standing while dying, with his open arms upheld in prayer until the final moment. Saint Gregory, his biographer, recounts lovingly Benedict's last days in his *Dialogues*. It is appropriate to quote him here:

In the year that was to be his last, the man of God foretold the day of his most holy death to some of his disciples living with him and to others living at a further distance. In mentioning it to those who were with him in the monastery, he bound them to complete secrecy. And to those who were a distance away, he informed them of the special sign they would receive when his soul would leave his body.

Six days before his death he gave orders for his tomb to be dug. Soon after, he [Benedict] was seized by a strong fever and was made weak by a severe illness. Day by day his illness grew worse, so on the sixth day he asked his monks to carry him into the oratory, where he asked to receive the Body and Blood of the Lord to gain strength for the final departure. Then, while his weak body remained standing in the supporting arms of his monks, he raised his hands to heaven as he breathed his last.

That same day two monks, one of them in his cell in the monastery, and the other some distance away, received the very same revelation. They both saw a luminous road ascending in an easterly direction, a road made of rich carpeting and shining with many lights. The road stretched forward from the monastery in a straight line until it reached the heavens. And there in the midst of the brightness stood the figure of a man of glorious appearance who asked them, "Do you know who passed this way?" "No," they replied. "This," he told them, "is the road taken by blessed Benedict, beloved of the Lord, when he ascended to heaven...."

How beautiful, indeed, in the sight of the Lord, is the death of his saints! Like Christ, his master, Saint Benedict dies while at prayer, with his hands outstretched in the form of a cross. Again, like his master, Saint Benedict, six days before his death, ordered that preparations be made "in view of his burial," such as the anointing in the gospels. At the end, like his Lord and master, he announces in advance the hour of his death, and after his death he ascends to heaven in a glorious fashion that reminds us of the ascension of the Lord.

Saint John Climacus (MARCH 30)

Your abundant tears made the wilderness sprout and bloom, and your suffering made your labors fruitful a hundredfold; you became a shining torch over the world. O Holy Father John, pray to Christ our God to save our souls!

<small>TROPARION OF THE FEAST</small>

The Memorial of Saint John Climacus, kept today in this monastery, crowns and brings to a close the month of March in a very monastic fashion. Saint John Climacus, a true monastic teacher, is also commonly known as Saint John of the Ladder because of the famous book he authored, *The Ladder of Divine Ascent.* I understand that no other book, except for the Bible and some liturgical books, has been as many times copied, translated, or printed throughout the history of Christian spirituality as the book of *The Ladder.* It is a classic, not only for monks and nuns, but for all Christians. It is a book of timeless appeal. I often am in a state of delight when I discover an ancient version or an older translation and can compare notes with a more updated present-day text.

There was a time, not so long ago, when reading *The Ladder* was *de rigueur* for every monk. I wonder if this is still so in many monasteries, especially with the influx of so many new books with a more contemporary approach to spirituality appearing here and there. Sometimes I feel a bit left out, for my reading has not moved much beyond the seventh century: I have been immersed so long in the Fathers and the monastic sources that I never seem to have enough time to go beyond them and embark upon new reading. There is so much that I have not yet read of the early patristic period, and with such wealth there, I can't quite yet take leave from those early centuries. One day, I hope to be able to have time to read the

Cistercian Fathers. They fascinate me. There is a unique, pure monastic intuition in their approach and return to monastic sources. They also write with such grace, such beauty, and such style.

Returning to our saint of today, there is little known about the origins or the person that was John Climacus. There is an aura of mystery surrounding him, and that may be just as well. They write that he was a teenager when he embraced monastic life at Mount Sinai, in a monastery established close to where God revealed his face to Moses. There he shared with a small group of monks the life of *hesychia*, that is, a life of tranquil stillness. This provided him with more ample opportunities for deeper silence. He attached great importance to this. After making his monastic profession, Saint John retired himself to a small hermitage a few miles from the fortress monastery. It was in this state of solitude that he received from God the gift of tears and the grace of unceasing prayer. He remained in that solitude for forty years, except for a one-time visit to a large monastery in Alexandria. After forty years of desert solitude on the top of God's mountain, he was chosen by the monks of Sinai as the

abbot of the monastery.

It was during this time, as abbot of the large community, that he wrote *The Ladder of Divine Ascent*. He wrote it hesitantly, at the request of monks from another monastery. While he wrote his treatise with monks in view, he clearly transcended and extended his teachings to all of humankind. He was a true mystic, and many of the man-made barriers did not exist for him. He wrote:

God is the life of all free beings. He is the salvation of believers or unbelievers, of the just or the unjust, of the pious or the impious, of those freed from passions or caught up in them, of monks or those living in the world, of educated or the illiterate, of the healthy or the sick, of the young or the very old. He is the outpouring of light, the glimpse of the sun, or the changes of the weather, which are the same for everyone without exception.

THE LADDER, STEP 1

It may be of interest to notice that Saint John Climacus never sought to be ordained a priest. He was a monk, a seeker and a lover of God, and that was enough for him. Like many of the early monks who preceded him, such as Antony, Ephrem, Benedict, and many others, the mystery of his monastic vocation was enough to engage him entirely.

Saint Mary of Egypt (APRIL 2)

The power of your cross, O Christ,
Has worked wonders,
For even the woman who was once a harlot
Chose the ascetic monastic way.
Casting aside her weakness,
Bravely she opposed the devil;
And having gained the prize of victory,
She intercedes for the salvation of our souls.

LENTEN TRIODON, CANON OF SAINT MARY OF EGYPT

The life of Saint Mary of Egypt is not only an obvious ascetic triumph, a triumph of love, but also a triumph over any preconceived notions of holiness.

MOTHER THEKLA, *IKONS*

$\mathcal{S}$aint Mary of Egypt was one of those early Desert Mothers who has a timeless appeal to all those who seek God by way of the monastic life. Mary was a fifth-century prostitute from Alexandria who spent the early part of her life corrupting the young men of Egypt. She enjoyed entertaining all those who came her way, but she refused payment. Pleasure was the only motivation for her behavior.

One day she decided to join a group of pilgrims who were going from Cairo to the city of Jerusalem to celebrate the feast of the Holy Cross. With great curiosity she followed the pilgrims to the Church of the Holy Cross, wanting very much to see the true cross. However, a mysterious force somehow prevented her from entering the church every time she tried to do it. While the crowd of pilgrims could move forward, she felt paralyzed and couldn't move. Bewildered and saddened by her hopeless attempts to enter the church and glimpse the true cross and feeling utterly rejected, she turned to an icon of the Mother of God and prayed for help:

O ever blessed Virgin and Lady, you gave birth to the Word of God in the flesh. I know that it is not proper for me, foul and corrupt, to gaze upon your holy icon,

O most pure one! But if, as I have heard, God became man, born of you, to call sinners to repentance, help me in my distress, for I have no one to help me. Command the entrance into the church to be opened to me; do not let me be deprived of gazing upon the tree on which God in the flesh, born of you, was nailed and shed his own blood to redeem me. I call upon you to be my guarantor before your son that never again shall I defile this body with shameful fornication, but as soon as I venerate the tree of the cross, immediately after I shall renounce the world and all its vanities and I shall go wherever you, the guarantor of my salvation, order me to go and lead me.

And as Mary was praying to the Mother of God with such earnestness and tears, she received the grace to move forward to the cross of Christ, then forward to the River Jordan and forward into the desert, where the Mother of God led her, as Mother Thekla explains in *IKONS*, "forward into year after year of icy cold and burning heat, of temptation and carnal longing, of fear and despair, and, finally, of the peace above all understanding."

The example of the holiness of Saint Mary of Egypt, whose feast is celebrated on April 2, usually in the middle of our Lenten observance, has deep significance for all who follow the monastic way. Her life portrays the dramatic tale of the work of lust turned into the work of love by the mystery of grace and repentance. For the Christian who embraces the monastic state and receives the "habit of repentance," as the ancient monks used to call the monastic garb, it is the abiding conviction that humble repentance is his ordinary, real, and only way to God. Repentance is an illumination and a grace, a humble attitude of heart and mind that brings healing and inner freedom to all those who, moved by the Holy Spirit, embrace it wholeheartedly as a genuine gift from God.

The life of Saint Mary of Egypt is read every year in the Offices of the fifth Sunday of Lent in the Eastern churches and monasteries.

Open to me the gates of repentance, O Giver of life;
For my spirit rises early to pray toward your holy temple,
Bearing the temple of my body all defiled;
But in your compassion,
purify me by the loving kindness of your mercy.

Lead me on the paths of salvation, O mother of God;
For I have profaned my soul with shameful sins,
And have wasted my life in laziness.
But by your intercession, deliver me from all impurity.
When I think of the many evil things I have done, wretch that I am,
I tremble at the fearful day of judgment.
But trusting in your loving kindness, like David I cry to you:
Have mercy on me, O God, according to your great mercy.

"Lenten Troparia"

Saint Pachomius (MAY 15)

The fame of our father Pachomius and of his charity reached everyone. His name was heard even abroad and among the Romans, and they came to become monks with him. And the man of God Pachomius treated them well in word and deed, like a nurse comforting her children. When the men of the world saw Pachomius, a man of God in their midst, they were very eager to become Christians and faithful. For he was full of mercy and a lover of souls. And often when he saw men who did not recognize God their maker, he wept copiously by himself, desiring to save all humankind if he could.

The Bohairic Life of Saint Pachomius

Today is another positively beautiful May day. The blue sky is clear and cloudless. The air is crisp and cool, just the way I fancy for our work in the garden. Early this morning, I saw some orioles and goldfinches visiting the vegetable garden. They seem to find joy in that special spot. Everything else around the property seems to be dormant, in a state of perfect quietude. And, of course, there is beauty and serenity to be found in that stillness. The only negative feeling I have these days is toward a certain aspect of the weather: the lack of rain. We have gone now for twenty-five days without rain, and we are not sure when it will finally arrive. The weather forecaster mentions that perhaps next Saturday we may get some spring showers. But who knows? I am disappointed, for the gardens are suffering, in spite the fact that I water them every day. It is early in the planting season, and the water is needed desperately. Under such conditions, one cannot think

of transplanting anything in the garden, for fear of losing it. It is a rare thing to have water problems so early in the season. If it were July or August, I would not be so bewildered. Unfortunately, now is the moment when water from the heavens is more needed in the garden. If things don't change shortly, I will have to start another novena of prayers to Saint Joseph! Dear Saint Joseph, you are so often beseeched in this house, especially when a problem arises in our midst!

In the monastic calendar, we honor today the memory of Saint Pachomius, an early Desert Father and a pioneer of the primitive monastic movement. In our chapel, his ikon stands next to that of Saint Antony, symbolizing how much we owe to these two, our fathers in monastic life. Pachomius, like Antony, was Egyptian by birth, being born of pagan parents around AD 292. Perhaps one of the most touching episodes in Pachomius' life is the origin of his conversion to Christianity.

Being enrolled in the Roman army, he encountered a group of people that he came to admire greatly because of their inspiring charity toward everyone and their willingness to help those in need. Pachomius became curious and inquired who were these simple people, so selfless and heroic in their love for another. He soon found out the answer to his inquiry. He learned that these people were Christians, disciples of a master called Christ, who left as trademark to his followers that they must love one another as he has loved them. Right there and then, Pachomius decided that he, too, would become a disciple of Christ and a servant to others. For Pachomius, it was a moment of intense grace. He rendered thanks to God for the shining example of these simple lay Christians, who with their life deeds proclaimed the good news of their Savior and master, and with their example touched the innermost of his heart.

After leaving the army, Pachomius sought refuge with a humble Christian community. There, he received baptism and requested to be guided in his spiritual pursuit by a hermit named Palemon. Pachomius' intuition at the beginning of his conversion was to become Christ-like and serve humankind as Christ did. Afterward, he had a vision of God's grace passing through his hands and flowing out unto the entire world. This vision impelled him to spend the first three years after his conversion working and serving those most in need in the local villages. It is only after these three years of training in the "school of charity" that he felt moved to embrace the monastic life.

Deeply rooted in Christ's commandment of charity, Pachomius founded a monastic community that was based upon service and the practice of charity toward all. His fellow monks, following the example of the apostles, were to be united in love and to serve one another after the model of the first Christians. They were to be particularly known for their generosity and concern toward strangers and the poor. Pachomius' great gift and contribution to the monastic movement was being able to combine this insistence upon gospel charity with the most traditional monastic values practiced in the desert: silence, fasting, vigils, continual prayer, humility, obedience to the elders, study, and the reading of the Scriptures, among other things.

Pachomius was such an excellent monastic organizer that his monastery continued to grow to the point that he was obliged to found six other monasteries nearby, all of them under his spiritual direction. One of these new foundations was a monastery exclusively for women. Pachomius' own sister was the first to enter and later became the mother of the monastery. For all of them, the saintly monk wrote a simple Rule, just as Saint Benedict would do centuries later, to guide his monks and nuns in their continual search for God. The Koinonias, or monastery, founded by Saint Pachomius attached great importance to the role of the Scriptures and the Eucharist in their monastic life. The monks and nuns were fed by the word of God which they heard and chanted in their daily Offices, and by the Body and Blood of Christ, which they received at least once a week. Thus, the Pachomian monks and nuns strived to be of "one mind and one heart," and remained united perfectly in their communion in the word of God and the Body and Blood of Christ.

Saint Pachomius, humble monk and God's servant, died around AD 345, the victim of an epidemic illness that ravaged the Egyptian countryside. Before dying, he exhorted his monks to remain faithful to the monastic life they embraced and to seek in all things the perfection of charity. He died in peace, in the joy of knowing that he was going home to the Lord he faithfully followed and served for many long years.

CHAPTER 8
Summer Liturgical Cycle

Saint John the Baptist (JUNE 24)

Light in the flesh and Precursor of the Savior,
Offspring of a barren mother and friend of him
who was born of a Virgin,
You have worshiped him by leaping in your mother's womb
And have baptized him in the waters of the Jordan,
We entreat you, intercede with him, O Holy Prophet,
that we may escape from the mighty tempests to come.
FROM THE SYNAXIS OF SAINT JOHN THE BAPTIST

One of June's glorious events, a celebration that makes June an early-summer special, is the feast of Saint John the Baptist. It is a feast that brings great joy to this small monastic corner, hidden as it is in the vastness of God's universe. Monastics throughout the centuries have professed a particular affinity for John the Baptist. There are multiple reasons for this. He is a desert saint and thus a model for monks. He was particularly close to Jesus, the friend of the Bridegroom, in the same way a monk or nun aspires to be. He was dear to the heart of Jesus, who went as far as stating that, "No man born of a woman is greater that John the Baptizer." In essence, John was "canonized" by Jesus while he was still alive.

The passage in Luke's Gospel that recounts the birth of John the Baptist is one of the loveliest stories of that book. Fittingly, since John is Jesus' precursor, the story of his birth is told just before that of the birth of the Savior. This is the pedagogy of the Scriptures, the

Holy Spirit's special logic that arranges the sequence to explain one of God's greatest mysteries: the Incarnation of the Son of God. From the very first moment of his conception, John reveled in his unique relationship with the Son of God. Filled with the Holy Spirit, even from his mother's womb, he leaped for joy at the proximity of the Word Incarnate present in Mary's womb. Certainly, John the Baptist was one of the first to greet the arrival of the Savior into our midst.

From the moment when the angel announced John's conception to his father, Zacharias, the angel had entrusted a special mission to this child. He was going to be God's messenger. He would be the one assigned to prepare the way for the Lord. This unique role as herald of the Messiah is a role that John continues to play today. In the apse of our chapel we have a life-size icon of what is commonly called the Deesis. In the center stands the Christ Pantokrator, to his left and right sides are the *Theotokos* and John the Baptist making intercession for us. These icons speak volumes to me, for in reality, each day, I see the Mother of God and the faithful precursor pointing Christ to me, announcing him, speaking quietly into the ears of my heart about him, revealing his name to me. Daily they continue this work, this mission. And it is a double one, for not only do they point and speak to me about Christ, but they also speak to him about me; they plea and make intercession for me. Praying with the help of this icon makes each of the three—the Lord, his holy Mother, and John the Baptist—all are very present and very close in real life.

It is a given that one should pray to the Lord unceasingly, and that one should always count on the protection of the Mother of God. Few, however, think of imploring John the Baptist's intercession. Throughout the years I have become used to doing it in a very short and simple way. It helps me a great deal. Just as I make recourse to the Jesus prayer often, I also like to call upon the Mother of God often and with a short prayer: "Holy *Theotokos*, save us." And to Saint John the Baptist: "Holy precursor of Christ, intercede for my salvation." I repeat and repeat these very short invocations throughout the day, even when somehow far from the icon (though I do keep a small icon of the Deesis in the car, which helps me to pray when I drive). Through recourse to these short, simple prayers, the Lord, his Mother, and John the Baptist seem always present in the minutiae of daily life. In the icon, they gaze at Christ, and simultaneously they seem to look at me. For my part, I try not to wander too far or too long from their benevolent sight.

In the Eastern Church, every Tuesday of the week is dedicated to Saint John the Baptist. He is honored with the following troparion:

With praise the holy man is remembered,
Yet for him who has prepared the way,
The praise of the Lord himself suffices.
For you, O John, are higher in honor than the prophets,
Since you were chosen to baptize in Jordan stream him
Whom you foretold.

Solemnity of Saint Benedict (JULY 11)

To prefer nothing to the love of Christ.
     THE RULE OF SAINT BENEDICT, CHAPTER 4

The man of God, Benedict of Norcia, blessed in name and by grace, is one of those remarkable saints whose influence affected the course of history. He is called the "Father and Patron of Europe" because his Rule contributed enormously to the shaping of Western civilization. Saint Benedict was born in AD 480 in the small town of Norcia, north of Rome. During his adolescence he was sent by his parents to the great metropolis to pursue his studies. There in

Rome, Benedict encountered among the students a lifestyle of pleasure and vice and felt repelled. "Wishing to please God alone," as his biographer Gregory the Great points out, he decided to abandon Rome's worldly concerns and withdraw to the mountains of Subiaco, where he embraced a solitary form of monastic life.

After several years of strict solitude, a nearby community of monks approached him and requested that he become their abbot. Benedict accepted reluctantly, only to find later that this was a rebellious group of monks unwilling to accept any kind of reform. They went so far as to try to poison him. Benedict left the group and returned to his beloved solitude. Soon new disciples began to arrive, and he proceeded to instruct them both by word and example into the ways of monastic life. A new wave of hatred developed around him, and this time he decided to leave Subiaco permanently. He journeyed south with a few faithful disciples and settled in the area known as Monte Cassino, still inland, about halfway between Rome and Naples. In the new monastery, Benedict was able to organize the monastic life of his monks in accordance with his Rule for Monasteries. This Rule, according to his biographer, "is so remarkable for its discretion and clarity of style that anyone who wishes to know Benedict's character and life more precisely may find a complete account of his principles and practice in the ordinances of that Rule; for the saint cannot have taught otherwise than as he lived." Saint Benedict died around AD 547, leaving his Rule as a testament of gospel living for generations of monks to come. The Rule of Saint Benedict, full of wisdom and moderation and deeply rooted in the gospels, seeks to balance the daily life of the monks between practice of liturgical prayer, or *Opus Dei*, as Saint Benedict called it; the private, prayerful reading of Scriptures and the Fathers; manual labor to support the monastic community and physical rest.

For Saint Benedict, the aim of our Christian lives is to seek God and grow in the knowledge and love of Jesus Christ. The monk enters a monastery not to become a superior kind of being but simply to live his Christian life to the fullest. The monastery is, in Benedict's words, simply "a school in the Lord's service."

He counsels the monk to take the gospel as his only guidance, thus walking the path that Christ has cleared for all of us (Prologue of the Rule). The monk, for Saint Benedict, strives daily to become an ever humbler disciple who must prefer nothing to the love of Christ. The monk thus undertakes daily the work of love, particularly through prayer, which becomes the living expression of his love for God and neighbor. Expressed through prayer, love draws the disciple closer to his only master, Christ, and also to all that Christ loves, that is, the entire world and every single being in it.

The Transfiguration and the Assumption: Two Glorious Summer Festivals (AUGUST 6 AND 15)

Having uncovered, O Savior,
a little of the light of your divinity
to those who went up with you
onto the mountain,
You have made them lovers
of your heavenly glory.
Therefore, they cried in awe:
"It is good for us to be here."
With them we also sing unto you,
O Savior Christ who was transfigured,
And say: "Let us sing unto the Lord, our God,
for he has been glorified."
BYZANTINE MATINS OF THE TRANSFIGURATION

The month of August, caught right in the heart of summer, makes all of us a bit nostalgic. It brings back memories of past summers, of lovely holidays in the country, in the mountains, or at the shore. It reminds us of the endless happy gatherings with family and friends so typical at this time, of quiet strolls through the garden and the woods, of stopping at our favorite picnic spot. Alas, there is so very much for all of us to remember!

While August brings these deep personal memories to our minds, August also brings us the joy of the two great religious festivals of the summer: the Transfiguration of the Lord on the sixth and the glorious Assumption of Our Lady on the fifteenth.

The Transfiguration of Christ shows us the desire of the Father to glorify his Son before allowing him to undergo his passion. For a moment, the veil is lifted up, and Jesus appears clothed in unsurpassing beauty—so luminous, so resplendent, that the disciples participating in the event can instantly recognize that it is the glory of God shining in his face. From the midst of the clouds, a voice is heard: "This is my beloved Son, with whom I am well pleased; listen to him" (Matthew 17:5 *RSV*). These solemn words from the Father, nearly the very words already spoken by the same voice from on high at Jesus' baptism, bear witness that Jesus is the only Son of God, true God from true God, as we profess in the Credo. With one of the Byzantine hymns from the feast, we can sing,

Let us go up into the heavenly and holy mountain
Let us stand in spirit in the city of the living God,
And let us gaze with our minds at the spiritual
    Godhead of the Father and the Spirit,
Shining forth in the only-begotten Son.

The mystery of the Transfiguration contains an added hidden meaning: the cosmic transformation of the world at the end of time. Another Byzantine text reads, "To show the transformation of human nature at your second and fearful coming, O Savior, you did transfigure yourself! And you have sanctified the whole universe by your light."

Human nature, which is now under the spell of sin, will be freed and renewed when Christ comes in glory at the end of time. The light of Tabor, the light which shone from Jesus' face, sanctifies those who come close to him as the disciples did. It is also the light that nurtures our hope about the future of the world.

In the Eastern Christian tradition, the feast of the Transfiguration is also the feast of the harvest. On this day Eastern Christians keep the old custom of rendering thanks to the Lord of the harvest by bringing to the church and offering him their first vegetables, fruits, herbs, and flowers. Here in the monastery, after the liturgy we have the traditional blessing of the produce of our garden. This is a symbol of the earth itself being made new by the presence of Christ, rendering in homage its first fruits to its Lord and master.

The other great feast of August is dedicated to the Mother of God. On the fifteenth of August, we celebrate the Dormition, or falling asleep, of our Lady and her assumption into heaven. I find nothing better to describe this great mystery than to again have recourse to Byzantine texts, especially to the text sung at vespers:

What spiritual songs shall we now offer you, O most Holy Virgin?
For by your deathless dormition, you have sanctified the whole world,
And then you have been translated to the places above the world,
There to perceive the beauty of the Almighty
And, as his mother, to rejoice in it exceedingly.

O marvelous wonder! The source of life is laid in the tomb,
And the tomb itself becomes a ladder to heaven.
The Bride of God, the Virgin and Queen,
The glory of the elect, the pride of virgins,
Is taken up to her Son.

As we celebrate these two glorious and very monastic feasts of summertime, some subtle changes begin to be noticed in Mother Nature all around us: there are new arrivals in the garden, in the countryside, in the woods. August marks the appearance of goldenrod and loosestrife in our meadows and ponds, and the sound of the cricket rings stridently in our ears during the long, warm evenings. Among the August arrivals are the delicious blackberries, by this time well-ripened, peaches, plums, and early melons. Of course, the wonderful new corn is plentiful at this time.

With the arrival of August, we reach the peak of our seasonal garden work. Though it is hard and laborious, one feels deeply enriched by it. Our gardens have grown quite extensive throughout the years, and it is a full-time job to care for them. In the perennial garden, there is always something in bloom from early spring until late November. The other gardens are a mixture of annuals, biennials, perennials, and wildflowers. They fill the corners and borders with charming colors and delightful fragrances. One needs only to step outdoors to perceive the sweet scent arising from the beds of lilies, roses, and flowering nicotiana. Likewise, on the left side of the chapel, as one walks into the herb garden, one becomes inebriated with the strong aroma that arises from the herbs: lavender, mints, rosemary, thyme, and lemon verbena. This is particularly true in the early morning or early evening, or simply just after a rain.

Summer is an extraordinary season. It brings subtle changes in nature and calls forth growth and transformation on all of us. The lush exuberance and intensity of summer living has a profound influence on our human experience: our innermost thoughts, our intuitions, our interactions with others, our relationships with our own selves and with God. Summer gives us a vivid sense of the reality of living and instigates the continuous discovery of what living is for. When the summer days begin to wane in the monastery and the summer moon drifts away, we are ready to move forward into the next cycle, the quiet ripening of the seeds planted by the Holy Spirit in the soil of our lives.

Nativity of the *Theotokos* (SEPTEMBER 8)

Your Nativity, O Mother of God, has brought joy to the universe. For from you has shone forth the Sun of Justice, Christ our God. He has delivered us from the curse and blessed us. He has destroyed death to grant us eternal life.

TROPARION OF THE FEAST

Our summer celebrations culminate in early September with the lovely feast of the Nativity of Mary. It marks out this seasonal transition period, this "in-between" time.

Today's feast originated in the Christian East, where its celebration has the rank of a solemnity. The Nativity of the *Theotokos* is one of the twelve major feasts of the Eastern Church. Today's feast, therefore, is a source of gladness and joy for Christians of both the East and the West.

With her parents Joachim and Ann, we rejoice in the arrival of Mary into this world, for her birthday announces the proximity of another significant birthday, that of the Son of God. Today's festival is the one necessary event for the great mystery of the Incarnation to be accomplished. Mary proceeds forth in time from the bosom of her mother, Ann, in light, in gentleness, and in peace, ready to give her assent, her "fiat," to the Almighty One. In due time, she becomes the Mother of the Son of God. All of creation and the Church at large keeps this festival holy, rejoicing in the knowledge that Mary is in our midst and with her, the dawn of our salvation, the Sun of Justice, is nearer at hand, bringing with him the gift of redemption to all humanity.

Triumph of The Holy Cross (SEPTEMBER 14)

O Tree of dazzling beauty,
Adorned by Christ's precious blood.
he chose you as the royal bed
To rest his sacred limbs in death.
HYMN FOR VESPERS

Today is the feast of the Cross, a very special day in every monastery. I wish I could add "in every Christian household," but I fear that the secularized nature of our time attaches no importance to the mystery of today's feast. In the beautiful responsory sung at matins today, we sing: "The church venerates the glorious day on which the triumphal tree is exalted, on which our Redeemer, breaking the bonds of death, overcame the cunning serpent. Hanging on the cross, the Father's Word found the way of our salvation."

Today, our attention centers on the strange and wonderful mystery of the cross. On the day of our baptism, the sign of the cross was made over us as we were baptized in the name of the Father, of the Son, and of the Holy Spirit. The cross sealed our lives forever. From then on, we belonged to Christ.

Saint John Cassian (JULY 23)

Since you were open to God in all things,
You received the light of precious insights, O Holy father John.
Like the sun in high heavens,
You enlighten your devoted followers
With the wisdom of your instructions.
Now, remember all of us here below,
Fervently beseeching Christ, our God, to save our souls.

KONTAKION FOR SAINT JOHN CASSIAN

*W*hen I think of the evils of our times—war, intolerance, poverty, hate, discrimination, hunger, greed, cruelty, and materialism—I am reminded of the first Christian centuries, particularly of the times of Saint John Cassian, whose memory is kept

today in our monastic calendar. Those who have studied the history of that period have exposed that the then-fervent Christians, in their intent to preserve the integrity of the gospel, ended up by retreating to the desert in open rejection to the false values of the world of their times. Sometimes one naively wonders why this phenomenon is not repeated in our times and why are there no more people withdrawing to the desert today.

Although John Cassian left us a legacy of an incredible amount of writing, there are very few sketches about his personal life. It is said he was born in Dacia around the year AD 360. As a youngster, he was educated in the classics, which would serve him well later on. Fascinated by the monastic experiment in the Egyptian desert, he spent ten years there learning the basics of monasticism and receiving training from some of the renowned ascetics of his time.

Subsequently, he and a faithful companion named Germanus migrated to Constantinople, attracted by the reputation of its charismatic bishop, Saint John Chrysostom. In Constantinople, he was ordained a deacon by the saintly bishop. From Constantinople, Saint John Cassian eventually made a trip to Rome to confer with Pope Innocent and the Roman clergy, and while in Rome he was ordained to the priesthood. Not much else is recorded about specific events in Saint John Cassian's life.

During the time that Cassian spent in Egypt he became closely associated with Evagrius, who was a famous spiritual teacher in the Egyptian desert. Evagrius had a large following, John Cassian among them. After leaving Rome, John Cassian made his way to Lerins, in southern France, and there he founded two monasteries, one for monks and another for nuns, where he dreamed of perpetuating the desert monastic tradition as he inherited while in Egypt. Through the direct ties to Saint John Cassian, the monasticism of France can rightfully make a claim to an uninterrupted tradition going back to the Desert Fathers and Mothers. Through his writings, the Institutes and the Conferences, Saint John Cassian was able to introduce the monastic ideal to the West, especially the tradition of inner prayer as it has been previously practiced and lived in the deserts of Egypt and Palestine. For this, Saint Benedict and all the Western monastic Fathers are eternally grateful to Saint John Cassian.

Today, we see in our midst a renewed interest in the works of Cassian, and this can perhaps prognosticate better hopes for monasticism in the future. Perhaps, too, new expressions of monastic life shall arise for a world and culture that has already radically changed before our eyes. The classic forms of monasticism, based on the model from the Middle Ages and a nineteenth-century renewal, served well through the twentieth century. But alas, the times are different now and they may call for simpler and more gospel-oriented contemporary expressions of monastic life. The return to the monastic sources through hermeticism, sketes, lauras, and smaller monasteries seem to be on the rise, if not deliberately then forced by the lack of vocations. In French one often hears: *Le Seigneur ecrit droit avec des lignes courbes.* That is, "the Lord writes straight with

crooked lines." I place all of my trust in the fact that the monasticism of the future rests in God's hands.

Therefore it is beneficial and proper for each person, in accordance with the orientation that he has chosen and the grace that he has received, to strive most zealously and diligently to attain to perfection in the work that he has undertaken. He may praise and admire the virtues of others, but he should never depart from the profession that he has once chosen.

14TH CONFERENCE: ON SPIRITUAL KNOWLEDGE

Saint Gregory the Great (SEPTEMBER 3)

He who desires God with his whole spirit certainly already possesses him who he loves.

SAINT GREGORY THE GREAT, GOSPEL HOMILY 30, 1

Today we celebrate the feast of a great father of the Western church. Gregory was renowned as the prefect of Rome before leaving all worldly cares aside in order to enter a monastery on the outskirts of the city. There he became a monk and a deacon, and eventually—because of his wisdom and holiness—he was chosen as Bishop of Rome. This election as pope came to him as a surprise, with a great amount of personal pain, but he accepted it as God's will. Gregory, above all, was a contemplative monk, and nothing was more painful than leaving the seclusion of the cloister, where his spirit freely breathed and expanded in the ways of interior prayer.

At the time of his election as pope, the city and its surroundings were in the midst of turbulence. There were plagues, famines, and all sorts of Church and political controversies. It was an enormous challenge to assume the papacy at such a trying time. But Saint Gregory, like Saint Basil of Cesarea and Saint Martin of Tours before him, belonged to that special type of church pastor who was first formed in the school of monasticism. And that, perhaps, was the best preparation for assuming such an enormous responsibility.

As pastor of Rome, his main concern was the care of souls and the good of the Church of God. He never forgot, however, that above all things, his initial call was to the monastic life. During his papacy, he surrounded himself with monks and tried, as much as possible, to follow the monastic observances. He remained faithful to prayer and to his great love for the *lectio divina*. Essentially, he remained a monk his entire life.

Gregory was particularly attached to Saint Benedict, whose Rule he professed under in his Roman monastery and whose life and miracles he described for all of us in his book, *Dialogues.* For this, all of us who live under the inspiration of the Benedictine tradition are eternally grateful. After the Rule, Saint Gregory's writings constitute the most precious documents concerning Saint Benedict and his sister, Saint Scholastica.

Saint Gregory put immense effort into building and expanding the Church of God, not only through his pastoral care, but also through his writings. He is often called the doctor of holy desires, for his writings are a sublime expression of the exact nature of the soul's craving desire for God. According to Saint Gregory, this desire, when purged of vanity and falsehood, can intensify so strongly as to enter into the possession of God. There is a statement in *Dialogues* that beautifully expresses this holiest of yearnings: *Anhelare, aspirare, suspirare* (to desire, to aspire, to long for with overwhelming desire).

The desire of God, for Saint Gregory, becomes the fundamental quest of all Christian life. It demands of us detachment and purification from all other forms of earthly desire so that all of our spiritual energies may be unified and directed solely toward God. It nurtures prayer, brings inner peace and harmony, and enlightens the soul in the knowledge of the eternal mystery of God.

CHAPTER 9

Autumn Liturgical Cycle

All Saints (NOVEMBER 1)

I saw a vast crowd of countless numbers from every nation, standing before the throne.

VIDI TURBA MAGNA, VESPERS FIRST ANTIPHON

As we leave behind the bright, golden October days and enter into November, the eleventh month of the year, we perceive a certain change in both weather and duration of daylight. Daylight savings time changes around the end of October, and, suddenly, we are moved into the cycle of shorter days and longer, darker nights.

November, with its somber days, is often reputed as one of the gloomiest months of the whole year. It is the time when we witness the end of the brilliant autumnal foliage. The luster of the maples and ashes on the monastic property gradually disappear, leaving only some rugged oak trees with leaves still grasping to their boughs. Later in November, frequent rains and gusty winds will thresh away even the hardiest of the remaining leaves. Nature has its own unmistakable way of telling us that the year's end is quickly approaching. As the poet William Hope once wrote:

Ah, the year is fleeing from us;
Bleak the day, and drear the night.

Just as we enter into our darker, chillier November days, the festival of All Saints arrives as a beam of sunlight into our bleakness. Like many of the great Church solemnities, the feast of All Saints is of great antiquity. There are indications that in the fourth century, some churches celebrated on this particular day the commemoration of All Martyrs. Later on, Pope Boniface IV consecrated a church in Rome to the Mother of God and all of the martyrs in the seventh century and requested that the anniversary of this consecration be observed each year as a feast. A century later, Pope Gregory III dedicated, in Saint Peter's basilica, a chapel to All Saints, and ordered that a festival be observed each November 1, the anniversary of the chapel's consecration. Thus, the festival was to be observed as the harvest of Christ's redemption, as a fitting conclusion to the church year.

The antiphons, hymns, and readings of today's Office carry us to the heavenly Jerusalem, to the throne of the Lamb, around whom the elect worship in jubilant adoration. *Vidi turba magna*: "I see an immense crowd." Vespers' first antiphon gives us a glimpse of that majestic crowd surrounding the Lamb. Such a glorious gathering is composed of God's friends, who, by the way, are also our own friends and intercessors.

The walls of our tiny chapel are filled with icons of the Lord, the Mother of God, the archangels, the apostles, the fathers, and monastic saints. To me, they represent "God's family," the *turba magna* of the antiphon. During the liturgical celebrations, oil lamps burn in front of them as humble homage and as symbol of our silent supplication. Contemplating their presence in our chapel, one is moved to comprehend something of that marvelous mystery which is the communion of saints. I consider this to be one of the most consoling mysteries of our Christian faith. "I believe in the… communion of saints," we profess in the Creed, and the reality of this mystery should be a source of great joy for all of us.

While on our earthly journey, there is no better company to keep than that of the saints. They pray without ceasing for us, and they are always ready to come to our rescue. Our great hope is that we shall one day join them, becoming part of that immense *turba magna*, singing with them the eternal *sanctus* in the worship of the Trinity.

You have shown your saints the path of life,
You have filled them with joy in your presence, O Lord.
MONASTIC OFFICE FOR ALL SAINTS DAY

Saint Martin of Tours: Monk and Shepherd (NOVEMBER 11)

Filled with joy, Martin was welcomed by Abraham. Martin left this life a poor and lowly man, and entered heaven rich in God's favor.
LAUDS ANTIPHON OF THE FEAST

Today we celebrate the feast of a truly monastic saint: Martin of Tours. Here in the monastery, his feast is like a ray of sunlight shimmering through an otherwise gray and obscure November day. It is a feast we keep with great joy. Saint Martin is one of those monastic fathers that I am attached to the most and whose life and example have had a great influence over my own life. Most people think of him foremost as Bishop of Tours, forgetting that before anything else, he was a monk through and through.

Sometime after becoming a Christian, Martin was inspired by the life of the father of monks, Saint Antony. Fired up by his example, he retired with his disciples to the solitude of Liguge, near Poitiers, where his friend, Saint Hillary, served as bishop. In Liguge, he founded a monastery that still exists today, in the exact same spot.

When Martin arrived at Liguge in 361, he and his disciples began to immediately emulate the life and example of the monks in the Egyptian desert. The Liguge monastic solitude was precisely what his spirit was seeking. During those years of intense prayer and deep silence, Martin became conscious of the strong workings of the Holy Spirit within him. He felt he was being prepared for a greater role in the Church of God.

Saint Martin can be considered one of the great founders and promoters of the monastic life in France, then called *Pays de Gaule*. He founded not only the monastery of Ligugé, but also that of Marmoutiers, near Tours, where he resided after being made bishop of the town. Throughout all of his activities as the prelate of Tours, he remained strongly attached to his monastic calling and made every effort to continue living as a monk.

As the pastor of the Church of Tours, Martin showed such a remarkable sensitivity toward all. This was attributed to his monastic formation. His biographer, Sulpicious Severus, wrote: "We have seen numbers of Martin's noble young monks made bishops.... For what city or church would there be that would not desire to have its priests from among those in the monastery of Martin?" The biographer goes on further to express the quality of pastoral care that Martin exercised in the delegation of authority in his ministry: "He displayed such marvelous patience in the endurance of injuries, that even when he was chief priest, he allowed himself to be wronged by the lowest clerics with impurity, nor did he either remove them from office on account of such conduct, or, as far as in him lay, repel them from a place in his affection."

Martin died in 397, surrounded by his monks and faithful, filled with an immense desire to go and meet God. Because of his extraordinary holiness, Martin became the first person to be canonized who was not a martyr. Up to that time, only those who had shed blood for their faith were recognized as saints.

Both France and the monastic movement owe much to Saint Martin, who tirelessly worked to spread faith and the monastic life within that country. It is not surprising to see today how many thousands of churches dedicated to Saint Martin are scattered throughout the French landscape.

Saint Martin, merciful and humble,
Remember how monastic life
Was cherished in ancient days.
Revive today its vigour and its growth,
That God may be glorified in all things.

    LAUDS HYMN (*MARTINE PAR*) BY SAINT ODO OF CLUNY

Thanksgiving: Feasts of the Harvest

Come, ye thankful people, come;
Raise the song of harvest home:
All is safely gathered in
Ere the winter's storms begin.
God, our Maker, doth provide
For our wants to be supplied;
Come to God's own temple, come,
Raise the song of harvest home.

    HENRY ALFORD (1810–1871),
    THANKSGIVING HYMN

*I*n the monastery, where the rhythms of the liturgy are deeply intertwined with the rhythm of the seasons, the arrival of the autumn months signals the end of the agricultural year. During September, and even more during October and November, the last of the rich crops are harvested and stored for winter use, freeing the land for a period of rest until the next spring comes around.

In early October it is a beautiful sight to behold the wheat and corn standing tall under a blue, cloudless sky in the nearby fields of the local farms. The gently rolling farmland of Dutchess and Columbia counties, and neighboring Litchfield County in Connecticut—with their stone-fenced fields covered with pumpkins, squash, potatoes, and the last of the ripe tomatoes—is indeed a sight to see. To this I must add another sight, quite prevalent in this region: apple orchards covered with fruit, and vineyards with pale and purple grapes lined in heavy clusters coming to full fruition and extending their sweet, ripe aroma to all those who approach close. During our early autumn months when the weather is perfect, our eyes truly feast on a banquet of beauty in the surrounding countryside: a tapestry of harvest fields, orchards and vineyards in the meadows, the glory of the maple trees in full color, the bright sunlight, and the crystal-clear intoxicating fall air!

In monasteries, as in other farms and households, there is a heavy round of activities related to the harvest and preparations for the upcoming winter. It is the time to consolidate the summer's gains and process the earth's produce in manifold ways. There are bushels of new potatoes, all sorts of squashes, onions, garlic, and apples to be stored away safely in the monastery cellar for winter consumption. There are the endless amounts of freezing, canning, preserving, jam- and jelly-making out of the fruits of the harvest. These are all time-consuming activities but necessary to those of us who make an effort to live from the work and products of the land. There are also the harvesting and drying of the kitchen herbs.

Harvest time is a period of richness and plenty. It behooves the monk to pay close attention to the immutable rhythms of nature's clock, telling him to set aside other occupations for later and concentrate on the laborious work of the harvest. Work in the flower gardens also continues during the autumn months, though less intensively than during the summer. October and early November is a good time to divide and transplant the perennials. There are also some plants that need extra care, such as tender plants that must be brought into the greenhouse so they can survive another year.

The liturgy, too, has its own rhythm of seasonal and festal celebrations that, in our northern hemisphere, are closely connected with autumn and the harvest. On September 14 we celebrate in the monastery the feast of the Triumph of Christ's Glorious Cross. On that day the winter monastic schedule begins, which includes the monastic fast that, except for Sundays and feast days, lasts until Easter. During this time monks keep the ancient tradition of cutting down on the amount of food consumed, a practice that becomes a bit more severe during Advent and Lent. Fasting is not viewed negatively by monks but more as a means to achieve a change of heart and bring the weakness of our nature under control. Monastic fasting tries to bring into balance the spiritual order and the natural order in the monk.

On November 1 we celebrate the solemnity of All Saints. This is a family feast, for the saints are God's friends and our intercessors. The saints are very real to monks, as we are profoundly rooted in the faith of the early undivided Church. At the beginning of our monastic life, each one of us receives a monastic name of a saint, who then becomes a model, friend, and protector. We monks believe that the saints in their home above never cease to intercede for us and to help us do our tasks on earth adequately and promptly. The communion of saints is a mystery that is indeed very real, very personal, and very comforting to the monk's heart. Deep inside we know that we are really never alone, for the Lord is there for us, the Mother of God is there for us, and our friends the saints are also there making strong pleading for us.

On November 11, monasteries celebrate the feast of Saint Martin of Tours, an early monk and bishop who spent his life evangelizing France. It is an intimate monastic feast, for Saint Martin, especially in France, is very much loved by monks and nuns. After the feast of Saint Martin, we move on to the annual celebration of Thanksgiving, when we make a point of setting aside a day to bless the Lord and show him our gratitude for the miracle of a good harvest. Thanksgiving provides us the occasion to thank God not only for the harvest but also for the blessings throughout the year. With Thanksgiving Day we reach the peak of the season of plenty and fruitfulness. After that the evenings begin to shorten in a quite dramatic way, and one senses the steady decline of autumn as it seeks to merge with the hastily arriving winter.

In the monastery, autumn stands apart. It is a season that allows us to see our lives reflected in the beauty of the land all around us. As the trees let go of the glory of their leaves, so, too, are we called to let go of our encumbrances and press ahead with our spiritual striving. And as we let go of all that is superfluous and unwarranted in our monastic lives, we receive from the Lord the gift of inner peace and the promise of eternal life.

May he support us all the day long,
Till the shades lengthen
And the evening comes,
And the busy world is hushed,
And the fever of life is over,
And our work is done.
Then in his mercy...
May he give us safe lodging,
And a holy rest,
And peace at the last.
    JOHN HENRY CARDINAL NEWMAN

GLOSSARY

A Monastic Vocabulary

Abbacy: The term of tenure of an abbot or abbess

Abbatial church: The monastic church of an abbey

Abbess: The mother and leader of a monastery of nuns

Abbey: A monastery ruled by an abbot or abbess

Abbot: The father and leader of a monastery of monks

Abstinence: An ancient ascetic monastic practice in which monks and nuns abstain from eating meat

Accedia: A state of despondency and lethargy, a distaste developed by the monk for his spiritual or monastic life

Advent: The liturgical season that precedes and prepares for Christmas

Angelus: A monastic devotion honoring the mystery of the Incarnation

Antiphon: A short text taken from the Psalms and usually sung before and after a psalm

Antiphonale: A book that contains the music (chant) and text for the hours of the Divine Office

Apatheia: A Greek term used by the Desert Fathers to indicate a state of being no longer controlled or motivated by passions

Apothegm: A short saying given by a Desert Father or Mother to a disciple; a sentence that is life-giving and full of wisdom

Archivist: The monk or nun in charge of the monastery archives

Ascetic: A person engaged in a life of asceticism

Asceticism: The practice of self-discipline and self-denial

Asperges: The ritual of sprinkling holy water on monks or nuns at the end of compline before they retire for the night and on Sundays at the beginning of the conventual Mass

"Benedicamus Domino": A monastic greeting between monks and also to those who arrive at the monastery

Benedictine: The blessing asked before a meal and at other occasions

Bow: A deep inclination of the body used frequently by monks as a sign of respect

Breviary: The books that contain all the parts of the Divine Office

Cantors: The monks in charge of intoning or singing alone parts of the Mass and the Office such as antiphons, hymns, responses, etc.

Cell: The monastic room or bedroom where the monk lives alone with God

Cellarer: The bursar of the monastery, who also is in charge of coordinating the work in the monastery

Cenobites: Monks who live in a community

Cenobium: The original word for "monastery"

Chapter: The body of monks, similar to a board, who meet at required times under the direction of the abbot or prior to discuss important matters concerning the life of the monastery

Chapter room: The room in the monastery where the monastic chapter meeting is held

Choir: The part of the monastic church where monks or nuns participate in the Eucharist and sing the hours of the Office

Clappers: Wooden instruments, used to call the monastic community to services on the last days of Holy Week, that are used instead of a bell

Cloister: An enclosed section of the monastic building often used for processions

Collatio: The small evening meal taken on fast days

Compline: The night prayer of the monk; the last hour of the Office

Conversatio: One of the vows made by the monk during his monastic profession by which he commits himself to follow the monastic way of life

Cowl: The choir habit of the monks, used for liturgical functions and ceremonies, that is worn on top of the regular habit

Desert: The birthplace of monasticism and its constant ideal

Desert Fathers and Mothers: The Spirit-filled initiators of the monastic movement

Discretion: The teaching of Saint Benedict and a characteristic monastic virtue that counsels the monk to practice moderation and balance in all things

Divine Office: The traditional term for the monastic Liturgy of the Hours that comprises vigils, lauds, prime, terce, sext, none, vespers, and compline and it is sung at certain precise times of day

Dormitory: A section of the monastic building that contains the cells of the monks

Doxology: A short prayer of praise to the Holy Trinity sung habitually at the end of the psalms and the hymn

Elder: The name given to senior monks who are usually well-versed and experienced in the ways of the spiritual life

Enclosure: The private section of the monastery reserved for the monks and nuns to foster an atmosphere of silence and prayer

Eremitical: Elements pertaining to the life of hermits or solitary monks

Eucharist: The celebration of the Lord's Supper; also called the Liturgy of the Mass

Gardener: The monk in charge of the monastery gardens

Graduale: The book that contains the chants for the proper and the Ordinary of the Mass

Great Silence: The time of strict silence at night between the compline and the end of lauds

Gregorian Chant: The monodonic and rhythmically free Latin chant used habitually in the monastic liturgical services that has also been adopted to the English language by some monasteries

Guesthouse: The portion of the monastic building assigned to outside guests

Guest master: The monk assigned to care for monastery guests

Habit: The monastic garb or clothing of monks and nuns

Hebdomadarian: The monk or nun appointed to lead the Offices of the week

Hermit: A monk who lives in solitude

Hermitess: A nun who lives in solitude

Hesychia: Stillness, quiet, repose, tranquility. The inner state of constant prayer and union with God, it is the ideal of every monk and nun.

Holy water: Blessed water used daily as part of monastic ritual

Horarion: The daily schedule of the monastery

Hour: The name given to individual parts of the Divine Office

Humility: A virtue particularly stressed by all the fathers and mothers of monasticism

Hymn: A song of praise to God used at the beginning of each hour of the Divine Office

Iconographer: The monk or nun who has the task and gift of painting icons in the monastery

Icons: Holy images or representations of the Lord, the Mother of God, and the saints used in the monastery's worship or in the private devotions of monks and nuns

Infirmarian: The monk assigned to care for the sick in a monastery

Instruments of good works: Monastic counsels given in chapter 4 of the Rule of Saint Benedict

Introit: Entrance antiphon taken from the proper of the Mass and sung at the beginning of the eucharistic celebration

Investiture: The monastic ritual in which the novice receives the monastic habit

Invitatory: The Psalm (usually 94) and antiphon sung at the beginning of the Office of Vigils

Kalendas, Kalendarium: The listing by month and date of the liturgical feasts

Kyrie Eleison: A petition prayer meaning "Lord, have mercy" used in parts of the Mass and at the conclusion of the Offices. This short Greek prayer is one of the most ancient Christian prayers. The early monks used it as a method of achieving continual prayer.

Lauds: The second Office of the day, sung at dawn, is also sometimes called Morning Praise, for the psalms used in this hour are usually all psalms of praise

Lectio divina: A monastic practice of "reading the things of God," especially of the Bible, where God through the sacred text speaks directly to the monk's heart

Lent: The forty days of fasting and penitential practice that precedes Holy Week and Easter

Lessons: Readings taken from the Scriptures and from the fathers read during liturgical celebrations

Library: The special room in the monastery that contains all its books

"Listen": The first word of *The Rule of Saint Benedict*

Liturgy: The formal worship of the monastic community, which comprises the celebration of the Eucharist and the Divine Office

Lucernarium: Part of the Office of Vespers in which the first evening lights are lighted. It consists of Psalm 140, the prayers of the light, and the *Hymn of Light*. It is one of the most ancient parts of the Office, which the early Church inherited from the synagogue. It commemorates the evening sacrifice of Christ.

Magnificat: The canticle of Mary, sung every evening at vespers

Martyrology: The book that contains the sum of the liturgical feasts and the commemoration of the saints of each day is read daily to announce the feast or commemoration for the following day

Matins: The night Office or Office of readings, which today goes by an earlier name: the Office of Vigils

Metanoia: Repentance, conversion, change of heart

Missal: The altar book containing all the parts pertaining to the Roman Mass

Monastery: The dwelling place for persons who embrace the monastic life

Monastic: All elements pertaining to the life of monks or nuns

Monastic decorum: The personal etiquette, manners, or form of conduct appropriate for monks and nuns

Monastic fast: The period of fasting that monks and nuns undertake annually that encompasses September 14 until Easter, except for Sundays and feast days

Monastic profession: The rite by which the monk or nun engages himself or herself permanently to the monastic state of life

Monasticism: The establishment or state of life of monks and nuns

Monk: Comes from *Monos*, which means alone, single, solitary

None: The ninth hour of the Office, sung around 3 p.m.

Novice: The candidate for the monastic life who is being trained to become a monk

Novice master: The senior monk in charge of training the novices or new candidates to the monastic life

Novitiate: The period of time a monk spends in formal training

Nun: A woman who professes the monastic life

Obedience: One of the three monastic vows by which the monk renounces his own will and agrees to live under the direction of a Rule

Oblate: A person who is affiliated to a particular monastery and has a spiritual link to it

Observance: The particular practices of a monastery in following the Rule or ancient customs

Octave: The eight-day period following the celebration of a solemnity or major feast

Office: See "Divine Office"

Onomastic: The feast day of the saint for whom a monk or nun is named

***Opus Dei*:** Means "Work of God" and it is applied by Saint Benedict exclusively to the liturgical hours of the Divine Office

***Opus Manuum*:** Expression used by Saint Benedict referring to the manual work of monks

Oratory: The word used by Saint Benedict to describe the place where monks pray and chant the *Opus Dei*

Ordinary: The unchanging parts of the Mass and Office that are repeated at each of their respective celebrations

Parlor: The room or rooms in the monastery used to receive and speak to outside visitors

***Pax*:** Peace, the motto and ideal of monasteries that live under the Rule of Saint Benedict

Porter: The monk posted at the entrance of the monastery to greet visitors

Postulant: A newly arrived candidate to the monastic life

Prayer of the heart: Expression used to refer to inner prayer and more specifically to the recitation of the Jesus prayer

Prime: The first of the Little Hours of the *Opus Dei*, usually sung around 6 a.m. (It has been suppressed in the Roman Office and consequently many monasteries omit it today in their daily observance.)

Prior: The second-in-command after the abbot, and the superior in monastaries where there are no abbots

Priory: A monastery directed by a prior instead of an abbot

Procession: A liturgical ritual used frequently in monasteries

Profession: See "Monastic Profession"

Proper: The particular parts of the Mass or Office that change in consonance with the season or feast being celebrated

Prostration: A symbolic form of ritual of prayer used by monks that comes from the early desert tradition

Psalmody: The daily singing of the Psalms in the Divine Office, which has its origins in synagogue worship and that of the early Church

Psalter: The book of Psalms used daily in the Divine Office

Quies: Rest, quiet, stillness. The state of repose the soul enjoys when it is united with God.

Refectorian: The monk in charge of the refectory

Refectory: The dining hall of the monastery where monks partake of their daily meals

Repentance: Inner sorrow for sin; a deep desire for conversion

Responsory: Usually taken from the Psalms, the response sung during the Office after a lesson from the Scripture or a reading from the fathers

Rituale: The book containing all the established ceremonies of a monastery

Rule: From the Latin *Regula*, it is the book that is the guide for the life of monks and nuns. A Rule contains both the spirit and the prescribed legislation for monastic life.

Sacristan: The monk assigned to the care of the sacristy, vestments, and sacred vessels of the altar

Sacristy: A room attached to the monastic church where all the utensils connected with the celebration of the liturgy are kept

Sandals: Shoes consisting of soles strapped to the feet and usually worn by monks and nuns following ancient monastic practice

Scapular: A part of the monastic habit, worn over the tunic and hanging almost to the floor, that originated from the work apron used by monks

Sequence: A poetic hymn sung on special feasts during Mass before the Alleluia

Sext: The sixth hour of the Divine Office, usually said at noon

Silence: A constant monastic practice that encourages in the monk the spirit of recollection and continual union with God

Simplicity: A gospel virtue that encourages in the monk a state of being simple, innocent, and uncompounded, and frees the monk from false pretense and worldly cares

Solitude: The physical space where the monk or nun retreats from the noise of the world to seek God in quiet and seclusion

Spiritual Father or Mother: A monk or nun experienced in the spiritual life who serves as a mentor to beginners and those less experienced

Stability: The monastic vow binding the monk or nun to a particular monastery and community

***Statio*:** The monastic practice of assembling in silence for a few minutes in the cloister outside the church before processing inside for the celebration of Mass or the Office. This practice fosters recollection as a preparation for prayers.

Terce: The hour of the Office sung at the third hour of the day, around 9 a.m.

***Theotokos*:** The Greek word given to the Virgin Mary that means "Mother of God"

Tradition: In monastic life it means the handing down of teachings, beliefs, customs, and practices from one generation of monks to another.

Tunic: A simple slip-on garment, belted at the waist, which is the main component of the monastic habit

Versicle: A brief response sung during the Divine Office

Vespers: The evening hour of the Divine Office sung at sunset—when the first lamps were lighted in antiquity

Vigils: See "Matins"

Vow: A promise made to God

***Vox Dei*:** It means "the voice of God" and it is an expression given by monks to the ringing and sounds of bells that call them at appointed times to the worship of God

Weekly reader: The monk or nun who is appointed to do the reading during the coming week in the refectory

SELECTED BIBLIOGRAPHY

Saint Athanasius. *The Life of Saint Antony*. Baltimore: Newman Press, 1978.

Burton-Christie, Douglas. *The Word in the Desert*. New York: Oxford University Press, 1993.

Cassian, Saint John. *Conferences*. New York: Paulist Press, 1985.

Climacus, Saint John. *The Ladder of Divine Ascent*. New York: Paulist Press, 1982.

Cummings, Charles. *Monastic Practices*. Kalamazoo: Cistercian Publications, 1986.

D'Avila-Latourrette, Brother Victor-Antoine. *A Monastery Journey to Christmas*. Liguori Publications, 2011.

_____. *Blessings of the Daily: A Monastic Book of Days*. Liguori Publications, 2002.

_____. *Blessings of the Table: Mealtime Prayers Throughout the Years*. Liguori Publications, 2003.

_____. *The Gift of Simplicity: Heart, Mind, Body, Soul*. Liguori Publications, 2009.

_____. *Twelve Months of Monastery Soups: International Favorites*. Liguori Publications, 1996.

De Vogue, Dom Adalbert. *The Rule of Saint Benedict: A Doctorial and Spiritual Commentary*. Kalamazoo: Cistercian Publications, 1983.

Evdokimov, Paul. *The Struggle With God*. New York: Paulist Press, 1966.

Hourlier, Dom Jacques. *Reflections on the Spirituality of Gregorian Chant*. Orleans: Paraclete Press, 1995.

Leclercq, Dom Jean. *The Love of Learning and the Desire for God*. New York: Fordham University Press, 1960.

Levi, Peter. *The Frontiers of Paradise*. London: Collins, 1987.

Louf, Dom Andre. *The Cistercian Way*. Kalamazoo: Cistercian Publications, 1983.

Maria, Mother. *Sceptum Regale*. Library of Orthodox Thinking, 1973.

Merton, Thomas. *Contemplative Prayer.* Herder and Herder, 1969.

_____. *The Monastic Journey.* New York: Doubleday, 1978.

_____. *The Silent Life.* New York: Farrar, Straus, & Cudahy, 1957.

_____. *Thoughts in Solitude.* New York: Farrar, Straus, & Cudahy, 1958.

The New Jerusalem Bible. New York: Doubleday, 1985.

The Rule of Saint Benedict. Translated, with Introduction and Notes. A.C. Meisel and M.L. del Mastro. New York: Doubleday, 1973.

The Rule of Saint Benedict. In Latin and English with Notes. Ed. Timothy Fry. Collegeville: Liturgical Press, 1981.

Thekla, Sister. *Mother Maria: Her Life in Letters.* New York: Paulist Press, 1979.

Van Zeller, Dom Herbert. *The Holy Rule.* New York: Sheed and Ward, 1978.

Waddell, Helen. *The Desert Fathers.* Ann Arbor: University of Michigan Press, 1957.

Ward, Saint Benedicta. *Harlots of the Desert.* Kalamazoo: Cistercian Publications, 1987.

_____. *The Sayings of the Desert Fathers.* Kalamazoo: Cistercian Publications, 1975.